P

PSYCHOLOGY

TEACHER'S GUIDE

TALKING

POINTS IN

PSYCHOLOGY

TEACHER'S GUIDE

Rob McIlveen

Martyn Long

Anthony Curtis

Hodder & Stoughton

A MEMBER OF THE HODDER HEADLINE GROUP

British Library Cataloguing in Publication Data

A catalogue for this title is available
from the British Library.

ISBN 0 340 62120 6

First published 1994
Impression number 10 9 8 7 6 5 4 3 2 1
Year   1999 1998 1997 1996 1995 1994

Typeset by Wearset, Boldon, Tyne and Wear.
Printed in Great Britain for Hodder & Stoughton Educational, a division of Hodder Headline Plc, 338 Euston Road, London NW1 3BH by Athenaeum Press Ltd., Newcastle upon Tyne

CONTENTS

1

LEFT BEHIND BY THE RIGHT MINDED

1 A variety of explanations may be proposed by students and, no doubt, those who regularly participate in sporting activities will be able to offer interesting accounts of their own experiences. Without discouraging these, we would suggest that discussion of this talking point be firmly couched within established empirical research.

One study that students could be made aware of is that conducted by Wood and Aggleton (1989). These researchers looked at the representation of left-handers in several sports. Wood and Aggleton distinguished between two types of sporting competition. One type makes heavy demands on what they term 'rapid and accurate visuo-spatial coordination' and possibly confers an advantage on left-handers playing against right-handers because of the former's relatively unfamiliar style of play. Included here are tennis and cricket, and the researchers predicted that left-handers' strategic advantages, coupled with their possible innate neurological advantages, would result in them being overrepresented at the top levels of these sports.

Wood and Aggleton's second type of sporting competition also 'makes great demands on spatio-motor skills', but 'confers no automatic advantage for the rarer left-handed player'. Included here is keeping goal at soccer. Soccer goalkeepers were chosen by the researchers because, like tennis players and cricketers, they are required to make accurate responses to a fast-moving ball. In contrast, however, they should display no inherent 'side bias'. Wood and Aggleton predicted that if left-handers do indeed have intrinsically superior spatio-motor skills, a higher than expected proportion of left-handedness should be evident among goalkeepers.

The results of the survey revealed that there *was* an overrepresentation of left-handed bowlers in cricket. However, cricket batsmen, tennis players and soccer goalkeepers were not overrepresented. As Wood and Aggleton note, such observations cast doubt on the claim that left-handers have an innate neurological advantage in 'fast-ball' sports. The claim that, at least in tennis, there are more left-handers in the top half of the world rankings than would be expected (e.g. Azemar, Ripoll, Simonet & Stein, 1983) was also not supported by Wood and Aggleton's analysis of the data.

Although there might be a slight advantage to left-handed players in 'fast-ball' sports the effect is, Wood and Aggleton concluded, neither strong nor consistent. According to them, any advantage is tactical rather than the consequence of spatio-motor superiority. The left-handed tennis player Martina Navratilova (Navratilova & Carillo, 1984) has described a 'leftie advantage' when playing against a right-hander. The right-hander must change strategies when playing a left-hander. For example, the right-hander's strategy of playing a ball cross court to a right-handed opponent's usually weaker backhand will instead go to the normally stronger forehand side of the left-hander.

Left-handed bowlers in cricket may also enjoy a tactical advantage. They bowl the ball from a different angle and can move the ball in the opposite direction to a right-hander. Left-handed batsmen may enjoy success as a result of batting with a right-handed batsman, since the bowler must repeatedly change the line of his delivery and this often results in the length of the delivery changing as well. Fielders, who must change position when a right-handed and left-handed batsman take a run, might lose concentration and drop catches that would otherwise be taken (Eastwood, 1972).

Wood and Aggleton also discuss the tactical advantages of being left-handed in other sports. In boxing, for example, right-handers are relatively unaccustomed to facing a 'southpaw'. As a result, the right-hander must reverse his usual strategies for defending and attacking. The different stance of the left-handed boxer enables him to produce punches from different angles and directions to that of the right-hander (Porac & Coren, 1981).

In fencing, holding a foil in the left hand may also confer certain advantages to the left-hander. Perhaps unkindly, Sagan (1978) has noted that 'a malevolent left-handed swordsman might be able to come quite close to his adversary with his unencumbered right hand appearing as a gesture of disarmament and peace.' Students interested in pursuing the idea of left-handers taking advantage of their left-handedness may be interested to learn that some castles in Scotland had spiral staircases which were 'left-handed'. These castles were built by the Kerrs, a Scottish family evidently renowned for their left-handedness:

> But the Kerrs were aye the deadliest foes
> That e'er to Englishmen were known
> For they were all bred left-handed men
> And 'fence against them there was none.
>
> (Anonymous, reported in the *Journal of the Royal College of General Practitioners*, 1971.)

Research into left-handedness amongst those with the surname Kerr and its anglicised version Carr can be found in Shaw & McManus (1993).

2 Left-handers living in a right-handed world are clearly at a disadvantage with respect to many objects and utensils. Right-handed teachers and students may well be surprised by the number of objects right-handers take for granted which are difficult, if not impossible, for left-handers to use. Amongst other things, left-handers are disadvantaged with tools and equipment (such as saucepans and ladles with the pouring lip on the left), personal items (such as the winder on a wristwatch worn on the right arm), recreational items (such as fishing reels) and equipment used in schools (such as spiral notebooks and mounted pencil sharpeners). As one commentator has observed, whilst the left-handed hairdresser can now obtain left-handed scissors, he or she needs to 'stand on the left, competing for space with the right-handed operative next door. A left-handed haircutter in a busy salon is as rare as someone who thinks Graham Taylor [the ex-England soccer manager] should have kept his job' (Centipede, 1993).

For some writers, lateral asymmetries favouring right-handers exist at numerous levels, and this acts to disadvantage and put pressure on left-handers. As the article suggests, instead of receiving sympathy for being unable to use equipment, left-handers are marked down for clumsiness and ineptitude. This is known as the 'Right-sided world hypothesis' (Porac & Coren, 1981). Supportive of this hypothesis is evidence (e.g. Leiber & Axelrod, 1981) which suggests that, in the past, many, and perhaps all, left-handers have switched their handedness over time to fit in with the norm, that is, 'become' right-handed.

Given that many tools and other pieces of equipment are difficult for left-handers to use, it could be suggested that accidents occur when left-handers use right-handed implements in their non-preferred right hand. A poor grip or poor motor control could be the cause of 'clumsiness' and hence an accident. Perhaps even more important is the fact that left-handers have to interact with right-handers, who are not expecting opposite-sided reactions. Again, apparent 'clumsiness' in handing things over, collisions, and hence accidents, can result. This is the suggestion favoured by Bracha, Seitz, Otemaa & Glick (1987). The existence of shops specialising in left-handed equipment (see, for example, Lewis, 1994) could be discussed in terms of safety for both left- and right-handers! It is also worth noting that according to one study (Coren & Halpen, 1981) left-handers are five times more likely to die of accident-related injuries than right-handers.

3 This **Talking point** could be prefaced with a brief description of Geschwind's research. Geschwind was originally interested in the relationship between dyslexia and handedness. During a lecture to a group of dyslexics, he speculated that dyslexia might be linked to other disorders. After the lecture, several members of the audience spoke to Geschwind about the medical histories of their own families. A large number mentioned disorders like ulcerative colitis, rheumatoid arthritis, lupus and myasthenia gravis, which are known to involve the immune system. Instead of fighting infection by destroying foreign bodies, the disorders mentioned above cause the immune system to attack the body's own proteins in a case of apparent mistaken identity.

Students should be able to identify the male hormone testosterone as being, at least in Geschwind's view, causally related to handedness. Geschwind has proposed that an excess of (principally) testosterone slows the development of the left hemisphere as the foetus develops during pregnancy (and he suggests that 'maternal stress' may be the cause of the excess). In males, this would restrict the lateralised development of the brain, already a modification of an underlying female form (see Chapter 3), leading to both left-handedness and learning difficulties. Geschwind and Galaburda (1987) have additionally suggested that a surplus of male hormones has a negative effect on the development of the nervous system, and can lead to a higher incidence of immune disorders.

It is important for students to be aware that Geschwind's theory is not universally accepted. Additionally, Geschwind did not mean to imply that left-handers are in any way inferior or disadvantaged. In his view, right- and left-handers have different susceptibilities to different disorders, and left-handers may actually be more resistant than right-handers to certain infections and even cancer (Geschwind, 1983).

Students should also be able to identify preor neonatal brain damage as a suggested alternative causal factor in handedness. Different types of stressor might prevent the normal development of left-hemisphere dominance at a critical stage. Twins are certainly at a disadvantage since they are crowded in the womb, and the developing foetuses have reduced levels of oxygen and other nutrients.

It has also been suggested that a difficult birth, with associated anoxia (lack of oxygen to the brain), is causally related to handedness. The damage experienced at birth could shift cerebral dominance and handedness *or* prevent normal hemispheric specialisation. This suggestion can explain the higher incidence of left-handedness in pathological states like autism, subnormality and epilepsy, and (potentially) in terms of the incidence of left-handedness in the general population. It has been shown, for example, that left-handers are almost twice as likely as right-handers to have been born with a history of birth stress (van Strien, Bouma & Bakker, 1987).

At least some researchers (e.g. Iaccino, 1993) consider it extremely likely that an underlying pathological factor causes both an abnormality *and* left-handedness. Students should be made aware that at present, however, there is no conclusive evidence for any single cause of left-handedness. It does seem likely, though, that left-handedness *can* be the outcome of different factors in combination. Satz, Orsini, Saslow and Henry (1981), for instance, have proposed that what is inherited in left-handedness is a weakness for a lack of laterality which can be brought out by a range of different stressors. A useful recent review of handedness and developmental disorder can be found in Bishop (1990).

4 Students will probably have heard the expression 'cack-handed' used to describe left-handers, but may not know that 'cack' means 'excrement'. Sagan (1978) offers several examples of 'left-handed bad press'. In addition to the examples given in the article (affirmation and correctness indicated by 'right', important assistants described as 'right-hand men', and compliments with a nasty sting being considered 'left-handed'), the following may be noted:

a Anglo-Saxon: the word 'left' comes from 'lyft' meaning 'weak', 'broken' or 'worthless'.
b French: The word 'adroit' comes from the French 'a droite' meaning 'to the right'. As noted in the article the word 'gauche' means 'left' in French.
c Latin: 'Ambidextrous' means 'having two *right* hands'.
d Russian: The word 'nalevo' means 'left' and also means 'surreptitious'. 'Pravo' means 'right' and is a cognate of 'pravda' which means 'truth'.
e Italian: 'Mancino' means 'left' and also 'deceitful'.
f Mexican: 'Straight ahead' is translated as 'right, right'.

It is also interesting to note that pictures of the devil on tarot cards show the left hand being favoured and satanic rites (widdershins) follow an anti-clockwise direction. The devil originally sat on the left, and in St Matthew's gospel the devil's supporters (the cursed) are on the left while the chosen are on the right. To ward the devil off, we throw salt over the left shoulder. In the Talmud, the devil is 'Samael', derived from the Hebrew word 'se'mol' meaning 'left side' (Centipede, 1993).

5 Students will, of course, have their own views concerning this topic. It is worth pointing out that, at least in Britain, there is a far more liberal attitude now towards children using the left hand for writing than there was in the past. A review by Levy (1974), for example, showed an increase in children classified as left-handed from 2 per cent in 1930 to the current levels of 8–10 per cent. In several cultures, however, the lot of the left-hander actually continues to be far worse than that described by the article's author. In the Islamic world, for instance, there is an open and universal intolerance towards the left hand as the 'unclean' hand. Making primary use of it is considered an insult.

Sagan (1978) has tentatively suggested that pre-industrial humans (lacking toilet paper) used one hand for personal hygiene after defecation and the other for greeting and eating. However, Sagan's suggestions does not account for why the left and right hands were *originally* chosen for the different behaviours. If it was a matter of chance as to the roles of the left and right hands, then there would be an approximately equal number of societies using the left or right hand for hygiene and greeting and eating. This is not the case.

In a number of countries (the article mentions India), writing with the left hand is absolutely forbidden in the educational system (Thomas, 1989). In traditional Chinese society, for example, a strong social pressure is exerted for right-handed writing and eating. Teng, Lee, Yang and Chan (1978) found a nearly complete conformity in these two activities but little or no effect on handedness in other activities not subjected to special training.

Teng et al.'s findings go against the possibility (e.g. Collins, 1970) that handedness is due to the inheritance of a learning rule – a strong predisposition to choose one side or the other at an early age, with the side picked depending on chance or culture. The findings do, however, lend some support to the view that biological influences (perhaps those suggested by Geschwind) cause handedness: as noted earlier, left-handers have constituted a minority of the population since prehistory. There may well be students in the class from other cultures who have knowledge, and perhaps experience, of the ways in which left-handers are treated; their knowledge and/or experience may shed some light on the above.

Students should have detected the claim in the article (which uses King George VI as an example) that forcing left-handers to write with the right hand has been linked with the development of problems such as stammering (e.g. Corballis & Beale, 1983). As noted in 4 above, Geschwind has proposed that in left-handers, the left hemisphere's normal functioning is partially disrupted, and processing may therefore either be passed over to the right hemisphere or partly processed by both hemispheres. Because of the lack of lateral development in left-handers, confusion is caused in directional processing (since we read from left to right, new words are scanned in the right visual field and thus first processed by the left hemisphere). Consequently, 'b' is confused with 'd' (Orton, 1966).

Thus, it may well be disruptive to force obvious left-handers to adopt a right-handed writing pattern, and therefore children should not be encouraged to use a particular hand. However, since some left-handers have only weak lateralisation, this might *perhaps* be easily brought over to the right-handed norm. Indeed, there is some evidence to suggest that many left-handers do progressively adopt right-handedness over their life span (Porac & Coren, 1981).

6 It should be noted that the article does not cite evidence to support the claim that 'left-handers have more immediate access to the right hemisphere of the brain, which governs creativity and intuition'. It has been suggested that the brains of left-handers have a greater capacity for surprise and thus left-handers are able to see relations that escape more conventional brains (Fancher, 1979). However, and as Hassett and White (1989) have observed, 'to put it kindly, speculations of this sort have no scientific basis'. Although there are some highly creative left-handed individuals, population assessments (e.g. Lewis & Harris, 1988) offer confused and contradictory findings as regards the representation of left-handers. Left-handed students will no doubt disagree! The one exception to the confused and contradictory findings is in music. Lewis and Harris report that 16 per cent of musicians are left-handed.

With respect to the apparent overrepresentation of left-handers in mathematics, Benbow and Stanley (1983) found that 20 per cent of students scoring highly on the mathematics section of the Scholastic Aptitude Test were left-handed. A large-scale study conducted by Kolata (1983) found that mathematically gifted young children were more likely to be left-handed (and interestingly, as far as Geschwind's theory is concerned, were more likely to have a childhood history of allergies that involve the immune system).

Explaining the seemingly well-established overrepresentation of left-handers in mathematics is no straightforward task. Garmon (1985) has argued that left-handers are 'right-brain dominant' and therefore activities linked to the abilities of the right hemisphere are easier for left-handers to accomplish. In Garmon's view, left-handed people have better spatial reasoning ability than right-handers and it is this which accounts for their superiority in mathematics (but see also **7** below for an alternative account).

The data reported by Benbow and Stanley (1983) and Kolata (1983) have been challenged. One approach students could consider concerns subject choice and the established sex differences in handedness. In America (where both studies were conducted) males are more likely to enrol in mathematics classes. Since males are more likely than females to be left-handed, the increased representation of left-handers could be argued to simply reflect differences in interests and experiences.

7 Students should be made aware of the fact that laterality is seen by most researchers as having a long evolutionary history (e.g. Bradshaw, 1991). The **Background** to this chapter provides support for this, and additional evidence can be adduced from cave paintings of early hominids which show attacks on animals whose head wounds indicate the attack was right-handed. The possession of lateral specialisation has been most successfully accounted for in terms of an effective doubling of cerebral capacity; as each hemisphere performs a single type of task, it can do this better than if it had to be able to perform them all (Levy, 1974). There seems to be no plausible underlying explanation as to where the earliest form of evolutionary lateralisation originated from, although Bradshaw (1991) has speculated about the underlying basis being connected to the 'chirality' (handedness) of organic molecules.

One explanation for the development of left-handedness that has not previously been mentioned views it as a lack of development of laterality, particularly for language. A lack of development of laterality would lead to the involvement of both hemispheres in language with the partial displacement of the spatial ability which is normally present in the right hemisphere. Levy (1974) has suggested that this might lead to stronger verbal/sequential processing abilities in left-handers and could account for their claimed overrepresentation in music, law and mathematics, and their apparent underrepresentation in art and topology (the mathematics of shapes). Notice how different this argument is to that offered by Garmon in **6** above! Students could discuss the plausibility of these two very contrasting approaches and Annett's (1992) view that extreme right-handedness is related to poorer visuo-spatial skills – the *cost* of being right-handed.

Levy (1974) has also argued that the past evolutionary strength of left-handedness was to enable a few individuals in the population to engage in effective planning, which is a sequential process. Thus, this could have been one early advantage of being left-handed. The right-handed members of the group might have been better at tasks involving spatial abilities such as hunting (and perhaps this was an early advantage to being right-handed), but would have benefited from a left-handed group member's ability to plan and orchestrate the process or stratagem of the hunt.

Suggestions made by Beaumont (1974) could also be discussed at this point. He has proposed that the decreased lateralisation for language in left-handers is part of a more general difference in organisation. Right-handers are hypothesised to have few, more specialised, processing centres with correspondingly fewer lines of communication between them. A large number of processing centres in left-handers is hypothesised to have a larger number of weaker communication lines. This is an interesting model since it predicts differential task performance by right- and left-handers: right-handers should do well on simple, well-defined tasks, whilst left-handers should do well on complex and more loosely defined tasks. Beaumont's laboratory experiments have largely confirmed these predictions, although it is not certain how well they would transfer to broader, real-life situations.

With respect to the issue of determination, some researchers have argued that language developed from an existing right-hand dominance for sequential processing. Gestures by the dominant hand could have formed the basis for early communication, and paved the way for verbalisation. However, it seems equally as plausible to propose that early verbalisation and gestures existed together, based on even more primitive left-hemisphere specialisation for learned, sequential behaviours and the corresponding right-hemisphere specialisation for emotional and spatial behaviours (Bradshaw & Nettleton, 1981). Flowers (1987) discusses this issue further, although students should not be surprised to learn that the issue is far from being resolved.

8 Several ways of increasing the involvement of the right-hander's right hemisphere have been suggested. These include listening to music during lectures, using visual displays which act to present information as a whole, and getting students to construct 'mind maps' (Buzan, 1983). Some researchers (e.g. Edwards, 1979) have advocated approaches which prevent the right-hander's left hemisphere from being involved, such as copying objects which are presented upside down. Other researchers (e.g. Wheatley, 1977) argue that the right hemisphere can be involved in the less creative, more logical disciplines if spatial relationships are emphasised to a greater extent (by, for example, using various puzzles, mosaics and other geometrical forms).

It should be noted that some researchers have criticised approaches based on simply emphasising the right-hander's right-hemisphere processing. For example, Harris (1988) points out that virtually all tasks involve a close integration of both left- and right-hemisphere activities. Caine and Caine (1991) have therefore proposed that educational tasks should be constructed which emphasise *and* ensure that both types of processing are involved in an integrated manner. Such tasks would involve relevant and meaningful material within an overall and related context and process. Caine and Caine have produced a list of criteria for appropriate tasks. These include challenging and involving students, linking educational material to life experiences, using the physical context appropriately (music, layout, decorations, and so on), the development of social processes, and integrating and developing learnt material. Teachers using this book are, of course, already addressing some of these issues!

9 The item on the Annett inventory which is selected most strongly for right-handedness is 'hammering a nail into wood'. Many students who consider themselves to be right-handed will perhaps be surprised by the fact that the left hand is commonly used by otherwise right-handers to unscrew the lid of a jar and to deal playing cards. In order to assess hand *and* ear preference for listening to speech, students could be asked which ear they prefer when using the telephone. Do right-handers still keep the phone to the right ear when they want to write a message down? Which ear is favoured when listening to music through headphones?

Students could discuss their findings in relation to the various theories that have been addressed. Some may report a family history of left-handedness whilst others might have been told they experienced a difficult birth. It could well be that some students (right- or left-handed) use a 'hook-grip' in which the wrist is bent right over when writing. This is supposed to indicate that the same side of the hemisphere is language dominant (Levy & Reid, 1976). If so, such students *should* find that their preferred ear for speech is on the opposite side to their preferred hand!

References

Annett, M. (1992) 'Spatial ability in subgroups of left- and right-handers', *British Journal of Psychology*, 83, pp. 493–515.

Anonymous (1971) 'The handedness of Kerrs' (editorial), *Journal of the Royal College of General Practitioners*, 21, pp. 693–4.

Azemar, G., Ripoll, H., Simonet, P. and Stein, J.F. (1983) 'Etude neuropsychologique du comportement des gauchers en escrime', *Cinesiologie*, 22, pp. 7–18.

Beaumont, J.G. (1974) 'Handedness and hemisphere function', **in** S. Dimond and J.G. Beaumont (Eds.) *Hemispheric Function in the Human Brain*, London: Elek.

Benbow, C.P. and Stanley, J.C. (1983) 'Sex differences in mathematical reasoning ability', *Science*, 222, pp. 1029–31.

Bishop, D.V.M. (1990) *Handedness and Developmental Disorder*, London: Lawrence Earlbaum Associates.

Bracha, H., Seitz, D., Otemaa, J. and Glick, S. (1987) 'Rotational movement (circling) in normal humans: sex differences and relationship to hand, foot and eye preference', *Brain Research*, 41, pp. 231–5.

Bradshaw, J. (1991) 'Animal asymmetry and human heredity: dextrality, tool use and language in evolution – 10 years after Walker (1980)', *British Journal of Psychology*, 82, pp. 39–59.

Bradshaw, J. and Nettleton, N. (1981) 'The nature of hemispheric specialisation in man', *Behaviour and Brain Sciences*, 4, pp. 51–63.

Buzan, T. (1983) *Use Both Sides of Your Brain*, New York: Dutton.

Caine, R. and Caine, G. (1991) *Making Connections: Teaching and the Human Brain*, Alexandria, VA: Association for Supervision and Curriculum Development.

Centipede (1993) 'Fellow travellers of the left', *The Guardian*, 25 November.

Collins, L. (1970) 'The sound of one paw clapping: an inquiry into the origin of left-handedness', **in** G. Lindzey and D.D. Thiessen (Eds.) *Contributions to Behaviour-Genetic Analysis: The Mouse as a Prototype*, New York: Appleton-Century-Crofts.

Corballis, M. and Beale, I. (1983) *The Ambivalent Mind: The Neuropsychology of Left and Right*, Chicago: Nelson-Hall.

Coren, S. and Halpen, D. (1991) 'Left-handedness: a marker for decreased survival fitness', *Psychological Bulletin*, 109, pp. 90–106.

Eastwood, P. (1972) 'Studies in game playing: laterality in a games context', **in** H.T.A. Whiting (Ed.) *Readings in Sports Psychology*, London: Henry Kimpton.

Edwards, B. (1979) *Drawing on the Right Side of the Brain*, Los Angeles: Tarcher.

Fancher, R.E. (1979) *Psychoanalytic Psychology: The Development of Freud's Thought*, New York: Norton.

Flowers, K.A.F. (1987) 'Handedness', **in** R.L. Gregory (Ed.) *The Oxford Companion to the Mind*, Oxford: Oxford University Press.

Garmon, L. (1985) 'Of hemispheres, handedness, and more', *Psychology Today*, November, pp. 40–8.

Geschwind, N. (1983) 'Biological associations of left-handedness', *Annals of Dyslexia*, 33, pp. 29–40.

Geschwind, N. and Galaburda, A. (1987) *Cerebral Lateralisation: Biological Mechanisms, Associations and Pathology*, Cambridge, MA: MIT Press.

Harris, L. (1988) 'Right brain teaching: some reflections on the application of research on cerebral hemispheric specialisation to education', **in** D. Molfese and S. Segalowitz (Eds.) *Brain Lateralisation in Children: Developmental Implications*, New York: Guildford Press.

Hassett, J. and White, K.M. (1989) *Psychology in Perspective*, London: Harper & Row.

Iaccino, J. (1993) *Left Brain–Right Brain Differences: Inquiries, Evidence and New Approaches*, London: Lawrence Earlbaum Associates.

Kolata, G. (1983) 'Male genius may have a hormonal basis', *Science*, 222, p. 1312.

Leiber, L. and Axelrod, S. (1981) 'Not all sinistrality is pathological', *Cortex*, 17, pp. 259–72.

Lewis, S. (1994) 'A left-handed paradise', *The Daily Telegraph*, 19 March.

Lewis, R. and Harris, L. (1988) 'The relationship between cerebral lateralisation and cognitive ability: suggested criteria for empirical tests', *Brain and Cognition*, 8, pp. 275–90.

Levy, J. (1974) 'Psychobiological implications of bilateral asymmetry', **in** S.J. Dimond and J.G. Beaumont (Eds.) *Hemispheric Function in the Human Brain*, London: Elek.

Levy, J. and Reid, M. (1976) 'Variations in writing posture and cerebral organisation', *Science*, 194, pp. 337–9.

Navratilova, M. and Carillo, M. (1984) *Tennis My Way*, London: Allen Lane.

Orton, J. (1966) '"Word blindness" in school children and other papers on strephosymbolia (specific language disability-dyslexia)', *Orton Society Monograph*, 2, Towson, MD: Orton Society.

Porac, C. and Coren, S. (1981) *Lateral Preferences and Human Behaviour*, New York: Springer-Verlag.

Sagan, C. (1978) *The Dragons of Eden*, London: Hodder & Stoughton.

Satz, P., Orsini, D., Saslow, E. and Henry, R. (1981) 'The pathological left-handedness syndrome', *Brain and Cognition*, 4, pp. 27–46.

Shaw, D. and McManus, I.C. (1993) 'The handedness of Kerrs and Carrs', *British Journal of Psychology*, 84, pp. 545–51.

Teng, E.L., Lee, P., Yang, K. and Chang, P.C. (1978) 'Handedness in chinese populations: biological, social and psychological factors', *Science*, 193, pp. 1146–50.

Thomas, J. (1989) 'Implications of being left-handed as related to being right-handed', *paper presented at the Research Colloquia 'Issues in Education'*, Murray, Kentucky.

van Strien, J., Bouma, A. and Bakker, D. (1987) 'Birth stress, autoimmune diseases and handedness', *Journal of Clinical and Experimental Neuropsychology*, 9, pp. 775–80.

Wheatley, G. (1977) 'The right hemisphere's role in problem-solving', *Arithmetic Teacher*, 25, pp. 36–9.

Wood, C.J. and Aggleton, J.P. (1989) 'Handedness in 'fast-ball' sports: do left-handers have an innate advantage?', *British Journal of Psychology*, 89, pp. 227–40.

2

WHO IS THE REAL ME?

1 There are several advantages which can be gained by role-playing MPD. These include drawing attention to oneself or escaping responsibility for a socially unacceptable behaviour such as a crime. Students should be able to generate at least some of these. As the article suggests, at least one survey has noted that 'it was common among [apparent MPD] cases to attribute antisocial acts that they had performed to their other selves as a way of avoiding blame. In America, MPD has been used as a successful defence in rape and other serious crimes.'

The article cites the case of Kenneth Bianchi, the notorious 'Hillside Strangler' who was shown to be faking MPD in order to escape punishment for 10 sadistic murders he had committed. By seeing the characteristics of MPD portrayed in films like *The Three Faces of Eve* (which starred Joanne Woodward) and *Sybil* (an Emmy award-winning television drama starring Sally Field) it seems certain that a person motivated to fake MPD could do so.

Support for this comes from Rathus (1984). He notes that he has 'seen "mini-epidemics" of claimed multiple personality on psychiatric wards when patients had been confronted with socially unacceptable behaviour and found out that others were attributing such behaviour to other personalities dwelling within them'. As Rathus suggests, 'such evidence does not mean that there is no such thing as multiple personality; however, it does suggest that a number of individuals do attempt to escape responsibility by attributing misbehaviour to forces beyond

their control.' Other advantages that could be discussed are described in 3 below.

Students may be interested to know that the 'Hillside Strangler' was discovered by prosecution lawyers to have imitated a psychologist and knew enough to imitate a person with MPD. As the article notes, he was caught out when, after being casually told by a psychiatrist that most cases of MPD have three personalities, he promptly produced a third one on cue!

Kenneth Bianchi was later diagnosed as suffering from antisocial personality disorder. Cleckley (1976) identifies 16 primary characteristics of this disorder including 'superficial charm and good "intelligence", "absence of nervousness", "untruthfulness and insincerity", and "lack of remorse or shame" '. All of these characteristics would seem to be **a)** conducive to committing a horrible crime, and **b)** useful to fake another mental disorder in order to avoid detection for a crime.

2 As noted in the **Background**, alternate personalities differ in a variety of ways including body posture and tone of voice. However, and as most students will probably agree, these sorts of behaviour would be relatively easy for a person to fake. Osgood and Luria (1954) have shown that the Semantic Differential Technique *can* be used to establish whether a person has different affective systems, but again the possibility of faking could not be definitively ruled out.

In their study of 'Jonah', Ludwig, Brandsma, Wilbur, Benfeldt and Jameson (1972) used a variety of tests including objective psychological tests such as the Minnesota Multiphasic Personality Index (MMPI), the Adjective Check List, the MacDougall Scale of Emotions, and intelligence tests. Although it has been suggested (Keyes, 1982) that various personalities may show differences in both emotional and emotion-free (e.g. intelligence) tests, once again the possibility of faking could not be eliminated.

The **Background** notes that Ludwig and his associates demonstrated significantly different EEG recordings for the alternate personalities of 'Jonah', and students may suggest the EEG as a method of detecting the genuine from the fraudulent. In addition to Ludwig and his associates' work, Goleman (1985) has reported that evoked potentials (regular patterns of electrical activity in the brain in response to some controlled stimulus) may accompany personality alteration. Moreover, in one study in which actors *pretended* to have MPD (Putnam, 1984), changes in EEG activity were *not* exhibited.

Unfortunately, in a study of two multiple personalities, Coons, Milstein & Marley (1982) concluded that EEG differences amongst the different personalities in fact reflected differences in mood change, concentration, and the degree of muscle tension rather than some inherent difference between the brains of normal people and those with apparent MPD. As Sue, Sue and Sue (1990) have noted in this respect, 'although the claimed evidence supports the existence of dissociative disorders, reliable methods to determine their validity do not currently exist.'

3 There are several ways in which Carlson and his colleagues' proposal can be tested. Berman's (1975) solution is, perhaps, the most straightforward. Berman suggests that genuine cases can be detected by **a)** learning if the split appeared *before* the therapy began and/or **b)** examining whether or not the reported personalities lead 'separate lives' beyond the confines of the therapeutic setting.

With respect to the suggestion of 'elements of performance', Berman has this to say:

> There are good reasons for doubting the tales of split personalities: the therapist's intense involvement with their patients; their own belief in the reality of the splitting; the use of hypnosis and other methods of suggestion. While some cases might be fictitious, and while in others a therapist's expectations may

have unconsciously encouraged the birth of the personalities detected, I believe that true cases of multiple personality do occur.

Berman believes that the use of hypnosis in getting sufferers of MPD to switch from one personality to another indicates that the power of suggestion, along with the individual's desire to please the therapist, plays some role in transforming what Rycroft (1978) describes as 'severe, but less exotic, emotional responses' into 'much more interesting cases of MPD'. Carson and his colleagues have proposed that the distinction between 'true and genuine' and 'false and fraudulent' is actually a false dichotomy, and that MPD may reflect unconscious efforts by the person involved to play various roles (Spanos, 1984).

Students could also be made aware of the concept of *'iatrogenesis'* at this point. This refers to conditions or disorders produced by a physician or therapist through mechanisms such as selective attention, reinforcement, and expectations that are placed on the patient. Sue, Sue and Sue (1990) provide an excellent account of the ways in which the investigation of MPD may encourage the appearance of the disorders, and also discuss the controversies that abound over the diagnosis of MPD. The article itself can also be used in this respect.

It is also worth mentioning that some 85 per cent of MPDs are young females, and the vast majority of therapists older males. Prince (1905), for example, was 44 when he studied Miss Beauchamp, a 23-year-old neurotic. Miss Beauchamp is actually on record as pleading to be hypnotised by Prince, 'And I do want you, please, please, to hypnotise me again. You know it is the only thing that has ever helped me.' The possibility that Miss Beauchamp generated alternate personalities to retain Prince's interest in her cannot be ruled out! This certainly seems to be the line the author of the article is taking. As he notes, 'perhaps ... British psychiatrists do not act in a way that (leads) to the creation of multiple personalities in our patients. We fail to respond to the cues that might lead a distressed, suggestible patient ... to develop symptoms of MPD.'

4 The case described was astonishingly complex and, in reaching a guilty verdict, the jury appear to have accepted that 'Sarah' was suffering from MPD. Students should be able to use information from previous talking points in order to argue a case for or against a guilty ver-

dict and the plausibility of an appeal. The following, more detailed, description of the court case could be used by teachers to structure the discussion of this talking point.

The principal characters in the trial were Mark Peterson, a 29-year-old married grocery worker and 'Sarah', a woman born in South Korea but brought to the United States to be raised by adoptive parents. Evidently, Peterson had gone for a drive with one of the personalities called 'Franny', who was described as a cool and capable young woman and the basic personality. Franny allegedly told Peterson of her other personalities and, having parked the car, he told Franny to disappear and asked to speak to the 'fun-loving' personality called 'Jenny'. Jenny was then a willing partner to Peterson's desire for sex.

The central issue was whether Sarah simply regretted the fact that she had made love to Peterson in the back of his car, or whether she was suffering from MPD and Peterson, knowing this, had therefore raped her even though one of the alleged personalities had consented to intercourse. Peterson was charged with having sex whilst knowing he was taking advantage of a woman with MPD.

When Sarah was asked by District Attorney Joseph Paulus, 'Do you have any personal knowledge as to the events in the car?', Sarah replied, 'No I do not'. When Paulus asked, 'Who would be in the best position to talk about the events in the car that night?', Sarah replied, 'Franny'. Paulus then asked to talk to Franny. After bowing her head and closing her eyes for five seconds, Franny emerged. Franny was then sworn in, and asked to give her version of the events.

Franny claimed that she told Peterson of her personalities and he asked, 'May I talk to Jenny, the one who likes to have fun?' According to Franny, 'I said "Of course". I then went away and I assume Jennifer came out'. Peterson was alleged to have then put his hand on her thigh and asked, 'Can I love you Jennifer?' In a totally different voice from Franny, Jennifer described what happened in the car, 'He kept slobbering all over me. I seen it on TV – people wiggling like that. And when a person says that, it feels good. So I put my arms around his back and said "That feels nice" '. Asked by Paulus if it had felt nice, Jenny replied, 'No. But you're supposed to say that aren't you. It was on TV.'

Peterson did not dispute that intercourse had taken place. However, his defence was that he did not believe Sarah was mentally disturbed, and claimed she was a willing and knowing sexual partner who was 'putting on an act'. According to Peterson, 'She excited me, she was pretty. I asked if I could make love to her and she said "Yes" '. Peterson admitted that Sarah had talked to him about her other personalities, but claimed the he thought she was talking about her brothers and sisters.

When Peterson later rang Jenny, it was Franny who answered the phone. Franny told Peterson. 'If you wanted to have sex, why didn't you come to me? I am going to prosecute you, you bastard.' In court, Inam Haque, a psychiatrist, said in evidence that Sarah did not know until afterwards that her body had participated in sex. 'Later on', he said, 'other personalities did tell her what had happened. This is the mystery of MPD.' According to the prosecution, all of the personalities with the exception of Jennifer did not want to have sexual intercourse with Peterson.

Sarah testified that from childhood she heard the sounds of voices that seemed to be arguing inside her head. Franny, the cool and capable woman who appeared to be the basic personality, had been traumatised by finding the body of her adoptive father crushed by a car he was servicing. The prosecution claimed that neighbours had warned Peterson that Sarah was 'mentally ill'. However, Peterson's lawyer, Edward Salzsieder, asked the jury to consider how, if mental health experts took years to diagnose cases of MPD, a new acquaintance could be expected to know what was happening in a woman he had only just met. One witness for the defence, psychiatrist Darold Treffer, suggested that Sarah's various characters were encouraged by therapists who believed in MPD. Calling the disorder the 'UFO of psychiatry', Treffer alleged that Sarah was faking.

Immediately after the jury's verdict, Peterson sacked his lawyer and remarked, 'This could have happened to anybody. I don't think she is mentally ill.' Ask if he was sorry, Peterson said, 'What is there to be sorry about? Why should I feel sorry for her?'

In addition to Sarah, Jenny and Franny, the following personalities also testified: 'Emily (a playful six-year-old who likes sweets but would not testify until she was handed her teddy bear), 'Brian' (a bodyguard), 'Eleanor' (a prim and proper woman), 'Sam' (the creature referred to in the text), and 'John' (a keen fisherman who befriended Peterson).

5 The perspective described is that propounded by psychodynamic theorists. They see the dissociative disorders as involving 'repression', that is, the blocking from consciousness of unpleasant or traumatic events (Kopelman, 1987). When complete repression of these impulses is not possible (because of the strength of the impulses or the weakness of the ego), the dissociation or separation of certain mental processes is held to occur (e.g. Sue, Sue & Sue, 1990). Such separation is seen as being *advantageous* to the person concerned. In amnesia, for example, large parts of the individual's personal identity are no longer available to conscious awareness. This prevents the recall of unpleasant or painful experiences. In fugue, the amnesia is accompanied by the beginning of a 'new existence' (Paley, 1988).

Psychodynamic theorists see MPD as an extreme conflict between the different parts of personality which everybody experiences to some degree. As the article suggests, 'all of us have experienced our "minds going blank"', and all of us behave in ways which sometimes surprise ourselves ('I don't know why I did it') or others ('I didn't think you had it in you'). According to Bliss (1980), everybody has a number of personalities that exist on a subconscious level. Whilst, as the article suggests, critics of MPD argue that in disturbed individuals these 'become amplified in a manner that is only quantitatively, and not qualitatively, different from normal', Bliss and others would disagree.

For Bliss, the dissociation process occurs to such an extreme that the different parts of personality exist as if they were totally separate from one another. Psychodynamic theorists suggest that in MPD different parts of the personality are alternatively allowed expression and repressed. As noted, repression involves the ejection from consciousness of unacceptable urges or ideas. These are often sexual or aggressive. For Freud a person is not, of course, aware when an unacceptable urge or idea is repressed since repression occurs unconsciously. Freud saw repression as being a normal aspect of personality development which allows people to place certain conflicts behind them and move ahead. However, because intense anxiety and disorganisation would occur if the different personalities were allowed to coexist, each is 'sealed off' from the other (Braun, 1986).

It is interesting to note that Rosenhan and Seligman (1984) have reported that people who are particularly good at entering self-induced trance states characteristic of hypnosis, in which a second personality is generated, have typically been exposed to traumatic events during early childhood. Frischholz (1985) has suggested that the sub-personalities function as 'releasers', and serve the purpose of dissociating the self from emotional and traumatic events that cannot be otherwise escaped.

By generating other personalities to endure their trauma for them, people are able to cope with the traumatic events. In so far as this 'coping strategy' relieves the stress that would otherwise be experienced, the individual is 'able to use alternate self or selves as and when the need arises' (Baron, 1989). By creating new personalities in response to new problems, a person may end up with 'any number of different personalities' (Spanos, Weekes & Bertrand, 1985).

For psychodynamic theorists, then, MPD allows a person to do things s/he would really like to do but can't, because of the strong guilt feelings that would ensue. In cases where an extreme conflict between contradictory impulses and beliefs occurs, the separating out of conflicting parts of the self allows a person to carry out incompatible behaviour patterns without experiencing stress, conflict and guilt. In that sense, then, personalities develop as 'protectors', serving psychological functions such as expressing anger, discharging sexual impulses, and as 'keepers' of painful memories.

The psychodynamic perspective has been applied to Lipton's (1943) study of 'Sara' and 'Maud K.', which is described in the **Background**. It has been suggested that the development of 'Maud K.' enabled the original personality 'Sara' to gratify her sexual desires by engaging in promiscuous sexual relations without conscious knowledge and thus without guilt feelings. Lipton notes that the original personality's high-school friends reported that she was 'boy crazy' and was 'always chasing after some boy, often being rude to her girlfriends, dyed her hair red, smoked, and used Listerine to deceive her mother about smoking'. The original personality denied the claims of her high-school friends, but the alternate personality readily agreed and revealed the events in question.

At first sight, the psychodynamic perspective is appealing. However, there are other ways to interpret MPD. According to Social Learning Theory, dissociative disorders can be seen as conditions in which people learn *not* to think about disturbing behaviours or impulses in order to avoid guilt or shame. *Not* thinking could be regarded as negatively reinforcing in that not thinking removes the aversive stimuli of guilt and shame. Another idea related to learning theory students could discuss is that a person selectively attends to particular environmental stimuli when locked into a particular role, and these stimuli are different from those attended when occupying another role.

6 The therapeutic approach described in the text could be briefly illustrated by means of case-study. Keyes (1982) describes the treatment given to William Stanley Milligan who seemed to possess 10, and possibly as many as 23, different personalities. After standing trial for the rape of three women, Milligan was found not guilty by reason of insanity, the first case of a multiple personality being acquitted of a serious crime.

At the Ohio Mental Health Centre, Milligan was placed in the care of David Caul, a psychiatrist with considerable experience of treating MPD. In individual therapy sessions, Caul was able to fuse Milligan's personalities into one competent person. So successful was the therapy that Milligan was eventually permitted to spend weekends away from the health centre. Unfortunately, people still feared Milligan's potential for violent behaviour, and were openly hostile towards him. This caused Milligan's personalities to defuse again, undoing all of Caul's considerable efforts.

In Britain, a charitable organisation called The Jupiter Trust uses group therapy sessions to treat MPD. Most of those treated by the Trust experienced sexual abuse in childhood. The therapy involves getting people to recall the painful truths about their degrading childhood experiences. The rationale is that if sufferers of MPD admit to painful truths which they have previously denied, and if they are able to do this in the company of others who would not be shocked or disbelieve their stories, they will be able to come to terms with their traumatic past. This is held to provide a more 'problem-focused coping strategy' than the development of other personalities.

Behaviour therapy has also been used to treat MPD. Learning theorists argue that there is much to be gained by *not* having to face stressful situations directly. Behaviour therapy therefore involves reinforcing only the healthiest personality with both material and social rewards. As a result, other personalities are weakened (or extinguished) because there is no longer any pay-off in their existence (Kohlenberg, 1973). Family therapy and play therapy (for childhood MPDs) are other possible treatment approaches that students could explore. These are described and discussed in Sue, Sue and Sue (1990).

Students should also be aware of the fact that, at least according to some writers, MPDs are *difficult* to work with. For example, Coons (1986) discovered that three-quarters of therapists said they had feelings of exasperation, and half had feelings of anger and emotional exhaustion, when working with MPDs. Presumably, this is because at least one of the personalities is resistant to therapy!

References

Baron, R.A. (1989) *Psychology: The Essential Science*, London: Allyn & Bacon.

Berman, E. (1975) 'Tested and documented split personality: Veronica and Nelly', *Psychology Today*, August, pp. 78–81.

Bliss, E.L. (1980) 'Multiple personalities: report of 14 cases with implications for schizophrenia and hysteria', *Archives of General Psychiatry*, 37, pp. 1388–97.

Braun, B.G. (1986) *The Treatment of Multiple Personality Disorder*, Washington, D.C.: American Psychiatric Press.

Cleckley, H.M. (1976) *The Mask of Sanity*, St. Louis: C.V. Mosby.

Coons, P.M. (1986) 'Treatment progress in 20 patients with multiple personality disorder', *Journal of Nervous and Mental Diseases*, 173, pp. 515–21.

Coons, P.M., Milstein, V. and Marley, C. (1982) 'EEG studies of two multiple personalities and a control', *Archives of General Psychiatry*, 39, pp. 823–5.

Frischholz, E.J. (1985) 'The relationship among dissociation, hypnosis and child abuse in the development of multiple personality disorder', in R. Kluft (Ed.) *Childhood Antecedents of Multiple Personality*, Washington, D.C.: American Psychiatric Association Press.

Goleman, D. (1985) 'New focus on multiple personality', *The New York Times*, 21 May, C1 and C6.

Keyes, D. (1982) *The Minds of Billy Milligan*, New York: Bantam Books.

Kohlenberg, R.J. (1973) 'Behaviouristic approach to multiple personality: a case-study', *Behaviour Therapy*, 4, pp. 137–40.

Kopelman, M.D. (1987) 'Amnesia: organic and psychogenic', *British Journal of Psychiatry*, 144, pp. 293–8.

Lipton, S. (1943) Dissociated personality: a case-study, *Psychiatric Quarterly*, 17, pp. 35–56.

Ludwig, A.M., Brandsma, J.M., Wilbur, C.B., Benfeldt, F. and Jameson, D.H. (1972) 'An objective study of multiple personality', *Archives of General Psychiatry*, 26, pp. 298–310.

Osgood, C.E. and Luria, Z. (1954) 'A blind analysis of a case-study of multiple personality using the semantic differential', *Journal of Abnormal and Social Psychology*, 49, pp. 579–91.

Paley, A-M.N. (1988) 'Growing up in chaos: the dissociative response', *American Journal of Psychoanalysis*, 48, pp. 72–83.

Prince, M. (1905) *The Dissociation of Personality*, New York: Longmans, Green.

Putnam, F.W. (Jr.) (1984) **cited in** RM Restak *The Brain*, New York: Bantam Books.

Rathus, S.A. (1984) *Psychology*, London: Holt, Reinhart & Winston.

Rosenhan, D.L. and Seligman, M.E.P. (1984) *Abnormal Psychology*, New York: Norton.

Rycroft, C. (1978) **Introduction to** M. Prince *The Dissociation of Personality (1905)*, New York: Oxford University Press.

Spanos, N.P. (1984) 'Disavowed responsibility for action: demonic possession, hypnosis, and multiple personality', *paper presented at a meeting of the American Psychological Association*, Toronto.

Spanos, N.P., Weekes, J.R. and Bertrand, L.D. (1985) 'Multiple personality: a social psychological perspective', *Journal of Abnormal Psychology*, 94, pp. 362–76.

Sue, D., Sue, S. and Sue, S. (1990) *Understanding Abnormal Psychology*, Boston: Houghton Mifflin.

3

ARE HOMOSEXUALS BORN AND NOT MADE?

1 With respect to the issue of measurement, it should be noted that the identification of the INAH-3 cluster requires a skilled neuroscientist (which LeVay undoubtedly is). However, some have argued that LeVay is guilty of making the technique sound much simpler than it actually is.

Whilst both LeVay's and Allen and Gorski's data are highly statistically significant, the range of INAH-3 sizes within the groups is large. Thus, some of the male homosexuals had an INAH-3 cluster as large as heterosexual men. As Kohn (1992) has suggested, 'a small INAH-3 would not necessarily imply homosexuality any more than a height of five foot would necessarily imply femaleness'. In an article published in *Nature* the editor, David Maddox, wrote, 'the scatter of measured sizes suggests that nuclear size, if in any sense a "cause", is neither a unique nor an unambiguous determinant of homosexual behaviour.'

The issue of causality is vital to the discussion of LeVay's findings. LeVay argues that the structural difference *does* cause homosexual behaviour. However, it could be argued that the difference is the *result* rather than the cause of homosexuality. LeVay's argument that sexual orientation is determined and fixed before birth has also been challenged. For example, whilst the Sexually Dimorphic Nucleus (INAH-1) is on average two-and-a-half times larger in men than women (as is noted in the **Background**), these differences occur *after* birth rather than prenatally (*New Scientist*, 1992). At age two to three, there is a decrease in the number of

female INAH-1 cells whereas the number of cells remains unaltered in males up to the age of 45, but declines thereafter. Thus, if sexual differentiation of the brain does continue for several years after birth (as the evidence suggests), the role of social factors in determining homosexuality cannot be ruled out.

The lack of knowledge about the samples studied is another issue that is important to discuss. Although the homosexuals were known to be homosexuals, the remainder of the sample were only *presumed* to be heterosexual. Additionally, it could also be hypothesised that structural differences between homosexuals and heterosexuals are correlated with the frequency of sexual activity rather than sexual orientation. Finally, it could also be suggested that HIV was responsible for causing the structural difference. Without knowing more about the samples studied, definitive conclusions cannot be drawn about the causes of the claimed structural difference.

Students could also discuss the role of hormones in the determination of sexual orientation. Money and his colleagues (see, for example Money, 1980) have compared genetic females exposed to excessive androgens during foetal development (a disorder known as Congenital Adrenal Hyperplasia) with a control group of girls not exposed to excessive androgens. Even though the former group were raised as girls, they displayed more 'masculinised behaviour' (defined as a preference for outdoor active play) than the control group.

However, one methodological criticism that

has been made of this research concerns the measurement of 'masculinity', and this is discussed further in **4**. It has also been suggested that masculinised behaviour is more related to the child's experience of chronic illness and hospitalisation; it may well be that children with Congenital Adrenal Hyperplasia rebel against the intrusion of medical authority into their lives and this, rather than hormonal influences, affects their behaviour.

2 Students should be able to extract the necessary information from LeVay's article. LeVay argues that if a person's sexual orientation is biologically determined then the view that it is freely chosen and therefore 'sinful' becomes untenable. This would lead to 'a rejection of homophobia based on religious or moral arguments'. For LeVay, the status of homosexuals as a minority would also be unarguable. In America, this is particularly important 'where the constitutional protection of groups hinges critically on the "immutability" of membership in a group'. At present, LeVay notes, protection for homosexuals 'has been rejected by the US courts on the grounds that homosexuality is a "chosen lifestyle" and hence not immutable.'

There is another political implication that is worthy of discussion here. Traditionally, conservatives have preferred 'nature' to 'nurture' as an explanation for 'deviant' behaviour. LeVay's research has seen a reversal of this view, with conservative opponents of gay rights paradoxically arguing against LeVay's deterministic view! Supporters of LeVay's position such as the late Randy Shilts, a prominent gay author, have suggested that a biological account of homosexuality 'would reduce being gay to something like being left-handed, which in fact is all it is.'

Students should also be able to identify the negative consequences identified by LeVay. One of these is the notion that if an identifiable cause (or for some people what LeVay terms a 'defect') can be shown, then it might be possible to 'diagnose' homosexuality prenatally and 'cure it'. The suggestion that women bearing a male foetus should have hormone injections to guard against the risk of having a homosexual son has already been suggested by Gunther Dorner at Humbolt University, Berlin (*New Scientist*, 1992). The ethics of selectively aborting a foetus if it could be shown that its sexual orientation was going to be homosexual rather than heterosexual could form the basis for an additional talking point.

The former Chief Rabbi, Lord Jakobovits, has already called for genetic engineering to prevent the birth of homosexual children (Saumarez-Smith & Klein, 1993). Jakobovits' comments have attracted much criticism. Shortly after the comments were made on BBC Radio's *Today* programme, Chief Rabbi Dr Jonathan Sacks ruled discussion of genetic engineering off the agenda since 'homosexuality – like all other complex human traits – is the result of an interaction of genetic, environmental and cultural influences (which) cannot be produced or removed by scientific procedures' (quoted in Ezard, 1993).

This talking point can be linked with **5** below, in which a possible genetic basis for homosexuality is discussed. If there is a gene that predisposes a person to homosexuality, prenatal diagnostic tests might enable a woman to terminate her pregnancy if the foetus could be shown to be carrying the gene. If the parents decided against abortion, the child might grow up knowing that it had been labelled 'genetically gay', and this might lead to a self-fulfilling prophecy. Some would argue that this in itself is sufficient to justify banning prenatal testing. Moreover, a 'homosexual gene' (if it exists) might serve other functions that we do not know about. It could, for example, serve some sort of protective function. A general discussion of the moral and social consequences of the 'new' human genetics can be found in Wilkie (1993). Other issues include the potential for using genetic screening as a basis for discrimination in health insurance, life insurance, and as a basis for discrimination for employment.

3 Students should recognise that the existence of any 'treatment' method implies that what is being 'treated' is either undesirable and/or pathological. This is one of the reasons why homosexuals are against 'treatment programs'. Psychotherapy, using free-association, dream interpretation and 'talking through', with special attention paid to the confrontation of Oedipal conflicts, has been used. However, the success of psychotherapy has been limited. One reason for this is that many homosexuals have been pressurised into obtaining treatment rather than voluntarily seeking it.

Behaviour therapy typically involves giving an electric shock to a person aroused by homosexual pictures or fantasies. The shock is terminated by either switching to heterosexual pictures or verbalising heterosexual fantasies. Another behavioural approach emphasises 'arousal reconditioning' and social skills training. The person is conditioned to become aroused to heterosexual stimuli, and is then taught how to meet members of the opposite sex with whom to employ the newly learned arousal pattern (Bootzin & Acocella, 1984).

Davison's (1978) position has been attacked by Sturgis and Adams (1978) who argue that the issue of whether homosexuality is abnormal or not is irrelevant. Sturgis and Adams argue that one consequence of Davison's argument is that therapists will impose their *own views* on whether an individual receives treatment or not. For Sturgis and Adams, any individual has the right to treatment. For Davison, no therapist has an absolute responsibility to provide what a client requests.

4 Operational definitions of gender nonconformity used by researchers include boys showing little interest in, or an aversion to, masculine activities like football or cricket, and girls displaying tomboy behaviours. Bell, Weinberg and Hammersmith (1981) found that only 11 per cent of homosexuals interviewed by them compared with 70 per cent of heterosexuals reported enjoying masculine activities. However, 46 per cent of homosexuals reported enjoying feminine activities compared with 11 per cent of heterosexuals. In women, 62 per cent of the homosexual group described themselves as having being masculine in childhood, compared with 10 per cent of heterosexuals.

The evidence suggests, however, that many tomboy girls and 'sissy' boys grow up to be heterosexual. If prenatal hormonal factors do influence gender nonconformity characteristics, and if prenatal hormones are the cause of homosexuality, then all tomboys and 'sissies' would be expected to be homosexual. It should be noted, however, that as mentioned in **1** above, the concept of 'masculinity' is difficult to define objectively. Some would argue that both 'masculinity' and 'femininity' are cultural concepts rather than objective innate characteristics, and have changed over time as ideas about what is appropriate to a particular sex have changed. With respect to self-report studies, students should be able to identify memory distortion as at least one of the dangers of relying on self-report measures. We do not know if this occurred in the people who were interviewed. It is well established that human memory often reconstructs the past to fit in with certain beliefs or schemas.

5 One reason for doubting a genetic explanation of homosexuality is the large body of evidence which has failed to find the strikingly high concordance rates that are described in the text (e.g. Rosenthal, 1970; McConaghy & Blaszczynski, 1980). Students familiar with twin research should also recognise that whilst monozygotic twins are genetically identical, they are also likely to have shared similar environments and experiences in childhood. A genetic account of homosexuality would only become more plausible if a high concordance rate was observed amongst identical twins reared in very different environments and subject to very different childhood experiences.

Another reason for doubting the validity of a genetic account is that whilst the concordance rates are impressive, none (with the exception of Kallmann's) has demonstrated the theoretically expected 100 per cent concordance rate. Note also that other work conducted by Kallmann on the genetic basis of schizophrenia has been subjected to much criticism (e.g. Marshall, 1984). Also worthy of discussion in this context is Heston & Shields' (1968) research. They studied a family of 14 children that contained three sets of male identical twins. Of the three sets, two were homosexual and one heterosexual. Students might like to explore these data in view of earlier discussion concerning genetic and environmental influences.

The recent research of Hamer and his colleagues (Hamer, Hu, Magnuson, Hu & Pattatucci, 1993) is also worthy of discussion. They studied 114 male homosexuals and found that their relatives (brothers, maternal uncles, and maternal male cousins) were more likely to be homosexual than would be expected among the general population, even though they were raised in different environments. This led Hamer and his colleagues to suggest a possible genetic basis for homosexuality.

The researchers studied the X chromosome, the sex-linked chromosome that a man inherits from his mother, in 40 pairs of homosexual brothers. Thirty-three of the pairs had inherited five identical gene markers, implying 85 per cent of families studied were passing on a gene responsible for homosexual orientation. Hamer and his team do not know why the other seven pairs did not appear to have the same genetic markers, but speculate that they could have inherited other genes concerned with homosexuality or might have been influenced by environmental factors or life experiences.

It should be noted that Hamer and his team accept that their discovery does not account for each and every cause of homosexuality, and they acknowledge that homosexual behaviour is most likely to be a result of the complex interaction of environmental factors, such as upbringing, and genetics. It should also be noted that the study was conducted on a group of 'self-declared' homosexuals and therefore not a random sample of the homosexual population. At the time of writing, there has been no search for the same section of the X chromosome in the heterosexual population, and no such genetic claim has yet been made for lesbianism.

Students may come up with some novel suggestions for the apparently paradoxical existence of a 'homosexual gene'. Discussion could be prefaced with a letter written by R.H.S. Carpenter, Lecturer in Physiology at the University of Cambridge, to *The Independent* newspaper (July 17th):

> If a gay gene exists, there is an interesting consequence. Other things being equal, a gene that vastly reduces the chances of propagating itself through reproduction will in the course of time gradually disappear. So other things are clearly not equal, and one is forced to conclude that the secondary effects of possessing the gene, either to those gays who do have children or to the society (gene pool) of which they form a part, are so beneficial that they balance the obvious reproductive disadvantage.

According to the sociobiologist Edward Wilson (1978), a genetic predisposition to homosexuality would confer an advantage to the *sisters* of the man because, in primitive societies, he would be less likely to set up his own home and more likely to raise his sisters' children. This so-called 'sterile worker' hypothesis has not impressed many people.

According to Richard Dawkins, homosexuals in early societies may have had access to females in the harem of a dominant male who believed, wrongly, that a homosexual male could be trusted not to have sex with his wives. According to Dawkins, since homosexual males do sometimes copulate with women, such a situation would have ensured the survival of a gene 'for' homosexuality. A second explanation offered by Dawkins is that any gene giving rise to a homosexual tendency may not have done so in our evolutionary past, when environmental upbringing was very different. However,

Dawkins has given no indication of what sorts of behaviours *might* have been involved.

6 One finding that would argue against a Freudian interpretation is evidence of the 'classic pattern' of family life occurring in *heterosexuals*. Since Freudians would argue that such a pattern does not permit successful resolution of the Oedipus Complex, the observation of heterosexual behaviour would be difficult for a Freudian to explain.

A second finding that would argue against a psychodynamic account of homosexuality would be the *absence* of the classic pattern amongst known homosexuals. There is evidence to suggest that at least some homosexuals have enjoyed excellent family relationships with both parents (e.g. Bell & Weinberg, 1978). Presumably, this relationship would be conducive to successful resolution of the Oedipus Complex. Interestingly, Bell, et al. (1981) report that the classic pattern only seems to emerge amongst those homosexuals who at some point have sought counselling or psychotherapy, and that whilst a poor relationship with the father is a significant predictor of homosexuality, it is only modest. The generally accepted view is that whilst family interactions might lead to some psychological problems later in life, there is not enough evidence to support the Freudian claim that family interaction is the causal factor in homosexuality.

With respect to the research reported by Bieber (1976), the sample consisted of 106 men undergoing psychoanalysis. The research could be criticised for studying *only* those homosexuals who had gone to a clinical psychologist or psychiatrist for help with emotional problems. It might be that such individuals are not typical of homosexuals in general. The interview method itself relies on the individual recalling events that occurred many years ago. As with Bell, et al.'s (1981) research cited in 4 above, recall from memory might not always be accurate. Students could discuss other disadvantages of this approach to data collection.

With respect to female homosexuality, the woman is presumably a) unable to overcome her strong attachment to the father, b) identify with the mother, and consequently c) proceed to the mature stage of genital sexuality, seeking partners of the opposite sex. Freudians term this 'faulty resolution of the Electra Complex'. According to the detailed study conducted by Bell, et al. (1981), the Freudian perspective has little basis in fact. Moreover, there is evidence to suggest that male and female homosexuality are not psychological obverses of one another. Sexuality is normally a dominant element in male homosexual relationships, whereas in female homosexual relationships emotional support and philosophical/political compatibility seem to be most important (Carson, Butcher & Coleman, 1988).

In the absence of any evidence concerning childhood experiences, it could be claimed that the relationship between homosexuality and an unhappy childhood was either **a)** entirely spurious or **b)** of the reverse type, with homosexuality being the *cause* of an unhappy childhood rather than the result of it. Whatever, as LeVay notes in his article, 'within a homophobic society, [Freud's theory] placed an undeserved burden of guilt on the parents of gays and lesbians.'

7 A large number of research findings can be used to claim support for a social learning perspective on homosexuality. For example, Hedblom (1973) has reported that many male and female homosexuals had enjoyable homosexual relationships before the age of 19, which could be taken as supporting the view that homosexuality occurs through positive reinforcement. Research conducted by Storms (1981) also supports the view that some people learn to associate their emerging sexual impulses with members of their own sex, and consequently develop homosexual tendencies.

Storms suggests that the relative availability of members of each sex is the main factor in determining sexual orientation. According to Storms, people attending schools that segregate the two sexes would be expected to be more likely to develop homosexual tendencies than those in coeducational schools. There is, however, no empirical evidence to support this proposition, but it could provoke lively discussion amongst students!

Learning theorists would also predict that males who had unpleasant experiences with females, such as being ridiculed, rebuffed or humiliated, or even punished by their parents for playing with members of the opposite sex, would tend to avoid females. If such avoidance was also coupled with sexual satisfaction from a member of the same sex, then homosexual behaviour would be predicted to occur. Note that some writers talk of this approach as 'social' learning. Strictly speaking, social learning involves the *observation* of others (termed 'vicarious' learning). Although the account

described above involves learning in a social context, it is simple operant conditioning.

Perhaps the most obvious findings that would argue against a behavioural perspective would be **a)** the perception of homosexual experiences during childhood and adolescence as unrewarding by a person who continued a homosexual lifestyle in adulthood, or **b)** the experience of numerous homosexual activities in childhood by a person who never doubted his/her own sexual orientation. Both of these findings have been reported (e.g. Bell, et al. 1981). Bell and his colleagues have also reported that sexual orientation appears to be determined *prior* to homosexual activity. They suggested that the most important single predictor of adult homosexuality was the self-reporting of homosexual feelings which usually occurred three years before genital homosexual activity.

Students could also be made aware of cross-cultural and historical studies of homosexuality. In some societies, such as the Melanesians in the South West Pacific, all unmarried males engage in homosexual relations with the full knowledge of the community. However, after marriage they are expected to assume a heterosexual activity pattern, a transition they appear to have little difficulty in making (Davenport, 1965). Amongst the Sambia of New Guinea, Sambian male youths are taught that females are 'poison'. The males engage in prescribed unlimited fellatio. However, nearly all become heterosexual men (Stoller & Herdt, 1985). Those who do not are considered extreme deviants.

In certain instances, homosexuality has been encouraged among soldiers (such as in the French Foreign Legion). The view was taken that the men would fight more fiercely to protect their lovers (Churchill, 1967). All of these findings challenge a simple behavioural interpretation of the origins of adult homosexuality.

8 It has been claimed that, amongst other things, boys and men score higher in tests of mathematical reasoning and spatial relations, whilst girls and women score better on tests of verbal fluency and the interpretation of facial expression. As noted, some psychologists see these differences as reflecting permanent brain alterations caused by prenatal exposure to sex hormones (although students should be made aware that there is considerable opposition to this view).

A very simple prediction would be that homosexual men would score lower on tests of mathematical reasoning and spatial relations, but higher on tests of verbal fluency and the interpretation of facial expression, as compared with their heterosexual counterparts. Data supporting at least some of these predictions have been reported in several studies conducted in Britain and the United States (reviewed by Kimura, 1993).

Sandra Wittelson is a neuropsychologist who believes strongly that neurobiological factors are related to sexual differentiation in the aetiology of homosexuality. In interviews conducted with 32 lesbians, Wittelson found that 'the majority of female homosexuals have some left-hand preference.' Whilst Wittelson is not implying that all left-handed women are homo-

sexual, she believes her data reveal an 'atypical pattern of hemispheric specialisation' among the lesbians. Students familiar with the material in Chapter 1, could attempt to link it to Wittelson's claims.

For Wittelson, homosexual men should be more likely to be left-handed than heterosexual men (as a result of being exposed to unusually low levels of prenatal masculinising hormones: cf. Geschwind's theory described in Chapter 1). However, in 38 homosexual men and a sample of the 'general population', Wittelson was unable to report a statistically significant difference between the groups with respect to right- and left-handedness (*New Scientist*, 1992).

References

Bell, A.P. and Weinberg, M.S. (1978) *Homosexualities: A study of Diversities Among Men and Women*, New York: Simon & Schuster.

Bell, A.P., Weinberg, M.S. and Hammersmith, S.K. (1981) *Sexual Preference: Its Development in Men and Women*, Bloomington: Indiana University Press.

Bieber, I. (1976) 'A discussion of "homosexuality": the ethical challenge', *Journal of Consulting and Clinical Psychology*, 44, pp. 163–6.

Bootzin, R.R. and Acocella, J.R. (1984) *Abnormal Psychology: Current Perspectives*, New York: Random House.

Carson, R.C., Butcher, J.N. and Coleman, J.C. (1988) *Abnormal Psychology and Everyday Life*, London: Scott, Foresman & Company.

Churchill, W. (1967) *Homosexual Behaviour Among Males: A Cross-Cultural and Cross-Species Investigation*, New York: Hawthorne.

Davenport, W. (1965) 'Sexual patterns and their regulation in a society of the South West Pacific', **in** F. Beach (Ed.) *Sex and Behaviour*, New York: Wiley.

Davison, G.C. (1978) 'Not can but ought: the treatment of homosexuality', *Journal of Consulting and Clinical Psychology*, 46, pp. 170–2.

Ezard, J. (1993) 'Rabbi bars debate on "killing" gay gene', *The Guardian*, 29 July.

Futuyma, D. (1993) reported in *The Guardian*, 17 August.

Hamer, D.H., Hu, S., Magnuson, V., Hu, N. and

Pattatucci, A.M. (1993) 'A linkage between DNA markers on the X Chromosome and male sexual orientation', *Science*, 261, pp. 321–7.

Hedblom, J.H. (1973) 'Dimensions of lesbian experience', *Archives of Sexual Behaviour*, 2, pp. 329–41.

Heston, L.L. and Shields, J.S. (1968) 'Homosexuality in twins: a family study and a registry study', *Archives of General Psychiatry*, 18, pp. 149–60.

Kimura, D. (1993) 'Sex differences in the brain', **in** *Mind and Brain: Readings from Scientific American*, New York: W.H. Freeman & Co.

Kohn, M. (1992) 'Sex and the brain', *New Statesman and Society*, 27 November, pp. 31–2.

Marshall, J.R. (1984) 'The genetics of schizophrenia revisited', *Bulletin of the British Psychological Society*, 34, pp. 177–81.

McConaghy, N. and Blaszczynski, A. (1980) 'A pair of monozygotic twins discordant for homosexual behaviour: sex-dimorphic behaviour and penile volume responses', *Archives of Sexual Behaviour*, 9, pp. 123–32.

Money, J. (1980) *Love and Love Sickness*, Baltimore: Johns Hopkins University Press.

New Scientist (1992) 'Obscure origins of desire', published as a supplement to *New Scientist*, 28 November.

Rosenthal, D. (1970) *Genetic Theory and Abnormal Behaviour*, New York: McGraw-Hill.

Saumarez-Smith, J. and Klein, Y. (1993) 'Rabbi in storm over "gay gene"', *Sunday Telegraph*, 25 July.

Stoller, R.J. and Herdt, G.H. (1985) 'Theories of the origins of male homosexuality: a cross-cultural look', *Archives of General Psychiatry*, 42, pp. 399–404.

Storms, M.D. (1981) 'Theories of sexual orientation', *Journal of Personality and Society Psychology*, 38, pp. 783–92.

Sturgis, E.T. and Adams, H.E. (1978) 'The right to treatment: issues in the treatment of homosexuality', *Journal of Consulting and Clinical Psychology*, 46, pp. 165–9.

Wilkie, T. (1993) *Perilous Knowledge*, London: Faber & Faber.

Wilson, E.O. (1978) *On Human Nature*, New York: Bantam Books.

4

A TWIN PEEK AT FAMILY FORTUNES

1 The point to be emphasised here is that for many psychologists the original question of 'how much?' has been replaced by questions which ask 'to what extent?' or 'in what ways?'. Whilst these reformulations are subtle, they are also intentional, and illustrate a profound conceptual revolution which traditional nativists and empirists have been forced to take in order to understand the origins of, and influences on, the human developmental life cycle. Nowadays, nature and nurture are largely viewed as two sides of the same coin, with each influencing the course of the other.

Students may perceive the formulation, expression, and subsequent revisions of the nature–nurture debate to be more linguistic than psychological. However, it is worth noting that the implications of this go some way to understanding divisions that do still exist between nativists and empirists in terms of their methodologies, theories, and practices which have shaped psychology's existence. For example, the terms 'nature', 'genetics', 'heredity' and 'innate' are often used interchangeably. There are, however, deliberate differences between them in terms of the degree of 'causality' or 'determinism' that may be assigned to each: the terms 'heritability', 'genetically controlled' and 'potential' are clearly far from simplistic concepts.

Likewise, the terms 'nurture', 'environment', 'empiricism' and 'empirism' are sometimes used to refer to a variety of environmental, social and cultural factors which may influence the course of human development. Indeed, it is interesting that the term 'determinism' is rarely equated with empirists (who appear to be much more comfortable using the term 'influence'), and seems predisposed to be used by nativists. Nativist research may be used by 'significant others' to at best remove parental responsibility for the development of children, and at worst to employ such 'assumptions' and 'supporting' evidence to legitimate repressive social practices in the name of determinism:

2 The two questions dealing with 'alternative explanations' and 'methodological cautions' are intimately related. Methodological criticisms, which allow alternative explanations to be advanced for the high correlations between twins with respect to various psychological criticisms, abound. Kamin (1974) has been one of the most vociferous critics. With respect to the study conducted by Shields (1962), which is briefly referred to in the **Background**, Kamin makes a number of points. These relate to sample size, the standardisation of the tests employed, and experimenter bias. He also notes that Shields defined separation as being 'at least five years during childhood'. However, whilst some twins were separated at birth, in some cases separation had occurred at the age of nine or 10. Moreover, many twins had regularly contacted each other or lived in the same community. Seventy-five per cent of the sample had actually attended the same school.

More alarmingly, from a methodological perspective, one of the pairs, separated at birth, were reunited at the age of five and tested at the age of 40! According to Kamin, 27 out of the 40 pairs were brought up by relatives, with others either reared in foster homes matched by the adoption agencies responsible, or raised by acquaintances of similar socio-cultural levels. Kamin has also criticised twin studies on the grounds that they used volunteer participants responding to requests made by the researchers in the media.

Most textbooks (e.g. Gross, 1992) describe in detail the criticisms made by Kamin and others. Whilst some of Kamin's claims have themselves been criticised, they do offer pointers to at least some of the cautions that should be exercised before the data generated by twin studies are accepted unreservedly.

3 The author of the article is almost certainly describing the correlation coefficient. Indeed, this is more than hinted at when the author quotes Lykken's claim that there is a 0.7 correlation among identical twins reared apart, 'while brothers and sisters reared apart from their families had zero correlation.' Students may need reminding about the correlation coefficient. It gives an indication of the extent of the co-variance between two (or more) variables and is a measure of both the magnitude and direction of co-variance. The correlation coefficient ranges along a continuum from –1 (indicating a perfect negative or inverse correlation), through 0 (indicating no correlation), to +1 (indicating a perfect positive or direct correlation).

The validity of using correlational techniques in assessing the nature and extent of genetic influences on psychological characteristics could be discussed at this point, particularly with reference to intelligence. Atkinson, Atkinson, Smith and Bem (1993) provide a thorough description of how correlation may account for the extent of co-variation in the form of 'heritability estimates'. Atkinson and her colleagues emphasise the importance of viewing heritability as a 'population estimate' rather than an individual assessment.

The article does not address this technique, using instead its scale of nought to one to explain (without any apparent justification) features 'strongly controlled by genes and therefore hard to change.' Students could discuss the consistency of meaning within this phrase, particularly since it seems to imply an inevitable deterministic stance which is not supported by the inherent methodological weaknesses, and

the inappropriateness, of correlation when used as a measure of causality.

Claims that genes are the deciding factor in the determination of at least some psychological characteristics have been made by a number of researchers. Peter Schulman of the University of Pennsylvania has suggested that genes account for 50 per cent of the difference in what he calls 'explanatory style' – whether we are basically optimistic or pessimistic. Claims for other characteristics are described elsewhere in this chapter.

The most well-known research team investigating the role of genes is that based at Minnesota University and led by Thomas Bouchard. The team's study began in 1979 and is one of the largest ever conducted, using 105 pairs of identical twins from around the world. As noted in the **Background**, part of the study's attraction concerns the apparently curious specific characteristics that identical twins reared apart seem to share.

Bouchard has claimed that for a variety of behavioural traits as diverse as reaction times and religious attitudes, a large proportion of the variation among people is associated with genetic variation. The Minnesota team have claimed that 70 per cent of the variation in IQ test scores is accounted for by genes, 50 per cent of personality differences, and around 40 per cent for job interest variation. The Minnesota team have also suggested that their data do not indicate that parents (who might be worried about the quality of their child rearing) cannot influence traits, but 'simply that this does not tend to happen in most families.'

Quoting Sandra Scarr, the author of the article acknowledges that the environment may play some role in the determination of behaviour, though students will note that this acknowledgement is not elaborated on. Schulman's claim (see above) that 50 per cent of the differences in 'explanatory style' is accounted for by genes, could be countered with the claim that the remaining 50 per cent of the variance is *unaccounted* for by genetic factors! Although Schulman reported that identical twins were more alike in their 'optimism' scores than non-identical twins, even he has acknowledged that this doesn't necessarily mean there is a gene for optimism. He has, however, suggested that people may have genes for other abilities such as being well coordinated or outgoing, which act to build up a belief that the world is a rewarding place. One fact Schulman appears to have overlooked is that therapy can be highly effective in changing a person's outlook on the world!

4 We can offer no single answer to the question that has been posed! The purpose of the question is to encourage students to critically consider alternative methods and approaches to correlation, and to examine issues surrounding, amongst others, the following:

a the selection of an appropriate experimental design
b the specification of independent and dependent variables
c the operationalisation of variables
d the selection of an appropriate sampling method
e the control of possible confounding variables
f the collection and analysis of data

Such a challenge should encourage students to be selective, explorative, and reflective about the different methodologies that are available. A useful source for students to consider in this respect is Coolican (1994).

5 Before students enter into a discussion of the counters that environmentalists would make, they should be made aware that the claims made by Egeland and his colleagues have subsequently been withdrawn, largely on methodological grounds. Notwithstanding this caution, research has continued on larger scale pan-European projects. Discussion could be focused on the impact and subsequent influence of germs, genes, and chemicals on behaviour which, consistent with the medical model of abnormality, may see the latter as an inevitable consequence of the former.

Although the incidence of manic-depression among the Amish could be explained in terms of marker genes on chromosome 11, there are clearly many other factors which could contribute to manic-depression's aetiology. The non-materialist, low income, insular, agricultural and rurally dominated lifestyle of the Amish, as well as interbreeding, could all be used (to varying degrees of success) to counteract a genetic perspective.

6 The nature and extent of interactions between genes and biochemistry and their influence, if any, on the subsequent expression of behaviour is a controversial area in psychology (e.g. Carlson, 1987). Neurophysiologists, psychologists, genetic physiologists and, indeed, psychologists themselves have all made claims about the potential causes and consequences of specific genes in the production of particular chemicals and hormones. It could be that the relationship between genes and chemicals may be more constructively viewed as interactional and non-specific rather than linear and sequential.

Extending this to the expression of behaviour within a social context, it is self-evident that causal assertions themselves break down since behaviour does not occur in a social vacuum. Rather, behaviour is a product of biological, social and environmental factors. Similarly, an understanding of genetic principles may only provide us with models of, or predilections towards, behaviour, rather than deterministic ones.

7 On the assumption that students have some degree of familiarity with factor analysis, it may well be that they find their understanding of the rationale behind factor analytic methods more convincing than the methods themselves! Kline (1991) gives an excellent account of both the rationale and procedures involved. Briefly, factor analysis is essentially a statistical technique which attempts to identify the minimum number of factors which can explain or account for the total variability in a given behaviour. Using correlational techniques, a matrix of intercorrelations are produced between Test-Test scores and Factor-Test scores. This allows a researcher to identify 'high' and 'low' factor loadings on specific variables (Atkinson, Atkinson, Smith & Bem, 1993).

Earlier, the point was made that correlation merely provides a measure of partial co-variance. In factor analysis the emergent factors are merely a product of this process. The technique could be critically viewed as no more than a matrix of correlation coefficients which, through the process of reification, generates *psychological characteristics* which are then assumed to exist! Whilst factor analysis is a statistical technique, the interpretation of relevant factors is, by definition, psychological in nature. The potential for ambiguity and bias should be recognised by students.

It is also worth noting that different uses of factor analysis with the same variables yield factors which remain either correlated or uncorrelated, further adding to the problems of interpretation. The classic example that could be used to illustrate this is the debate concerning personality between Eysenck and Eysenck (e.g. 1975) and Cattell and Kline (1977). The

Eysencks favour the orthogonal method, whereas Cattell and Kline favour the oblique rotation method.

8 Phenylketonuria (PKU) is an example *par excellence* of the real substance of this debate, since it clearly demonstrates the need to use an *interactional* perspective. A recessive gene inherited from each parent causes PKU. The infant is unable to digest an essential amino acid (phenylalanine). As phenylalanine builds up in the body, the nervous system is poisoned and irreversible brain damage is caused. However, the application of strict dietary requirements may (at worst) partially or (at best) wholly offset the inherited defect. In this instance at least, then, a genotype does not necessarily determine a phenotype. Similar patterns may be established in the field of gender role development in general, and sex differences in particular. La Barba (1981) provides an excellent account of the role of interactional effects in gender role differentiation.

9 Since the physical structure of the brain is strongly determined by genetic factors, it could be argued that 'intelligence' is, at least in part, shaped by the *same* factors (Baron, 1989). The negative correlation *might* be explained in terms of 'efficiency': high scorers on intelligence tests might, perhaps, have brains which can accomplish the same amount of cognitive work with less physical effort.

However, and as Baron (1989) has noted: 'Such suggestions are at the present time speculative and more evidence is necessary before firm conclusions can be reached concerning the relationship between brain activity, the brain's physical structure, and intelligence'. Nonetheless, Baron suggests the findings 'are suggestive and point to an intriguing new technique for studying human intelligence, and for linking important psychological characteristics to basic biological processes'.

Despite Baron's enthusiasm, some teachers and students may have trouble with this talking point. All brains show localisation of function, but not all functions are inherited. For example, fundamental visual perception (a localised function) depends on early experience. The same is true of language, which is also localised

but the result of a genetic predisposition coupled with learning.

Other research that could be introduced and discussed is that which claims to have linked 'intelligence' to the size of a person's brain. Hymas (1993) describes research conducted by Nancy Andreason and her colleagues at the University of Iowa College of Medicine. The brains of 37 men and 30 women (average age 38, average IQ 116) were studied using magnetic resonance imagery after each of the participants had taken an IQ test. When measurements were adjusted to take account of the differences in body size, the data indicated that around 33 per cent of the difference in IQ scores could be accounted for in terms of brain size or its sub-regions. Whilst the correlation was 'modest', it was significant, and the researchers concluded that the larger the brain the higher the IQ.

At first sight such a finding *appears* to suggest that 'quantity' rather than 'quality' of brain tissue accounts for IQ differences. However, even Andreason has conceded that 'the results [have] to be treated with caution as other factors related to "quantity" of brain tissue are important.' Other research described by Hymas (conducted by Tony Vernon and his colleagues at the University of Western Ontario) has claimed that the brain size of women is more related to verbal skills than spatial ability. Such claims have been treated sceptically. Helen Haste (quoted in Hymas, 1993) has suggested that 'IQ itself is a very crude measure of a range of different and complex aspects of intelligence ... [and] it is like trying to measure electrons using a twelve-inch ruler.'

10 There are many areas to which the nature–nurture debate could be, or has been, applied. These include personality, mental illness, aggression, leadership, language development and moral development. Discussion may revolve around the lack of precise operational definitions of respective nativist and empirist positions, together with the complexity of the interactionist position. An alternative approach may involve discussion which polarises the debate for specific issues (such as intelligence) based on the student's own personal experiences in the area in question.

References

Atkinson, R.L., Atkinson, R.C., Smith, E.E. and Bem, D.J. (1993) *Introduction to Psychology*, London: Harcourt Brace Jovanovich.

Baron, R.A. (1989) *Psychology: The Essential Science*, London: Allyn & Bacon.

Carlson, N.R. (1987) *The Physiology of Behaviour*, London: Allyn & Bacon.

Cattell, R.B. and Kline, P. (1977) *The Scientific Analysis of Personality and Motivation*, London: Academic Press.

Coolican, H. (1994) (2nd ed.) *Research Methods and Statistics in Psychology*, London: Hodder & Stoughton.

Eysenck, H.J. and Eysenck, S.B.G. (1975) *Manual of the EPQ*, London: Hodder & Stoughton.

Gross, R.D. (1992) (2nd ed.) *Psychology: The Science of Mind and Behaviour*, London: Hodder & Stoughton.

Hymas, C. (1993) 'IQ is linked to size of the brain', *Sunday Telegraph*, 18 July.

Kamin, L.J. (1974) *The Science and Politics of IQ*, Potomac, Md.: Lawrence Earlbaum Associates.

Kline, P. (1991) *Intelligence: The Psychometric View*, London: Routledge.

La Barba, R. (1981) *Foundations of Developmental Psychology*, London: Academic Press.

Shields, J. (1962) *Monozygotic Twins Brought Up Apart and Brought up Together*, London: Oxford University Press.

5

FANATICAL GURU OF BEHAVIOURISM

1 Students who have studied learning theory should recognise that Sutherland is almost certainly mistaken in his assertion. Skinner did not deny that behaviour changes in response to a stimulus – he simply classified this as respondent behaviour and argued that it was not as important as operant behaviour. Most general psychology textbooks (e.g. Gross, 1992) cover the distinction between classical and operant conditioning, and Sutherland appears to have made an elementary mistake. This is somewhat surprising given that Sutherland himself occupies an eminent position in British psychology.

In reply to Sutherland's obituary of Skinner, Blackman (1990) describes Sutherland as being:

> so petty in his anecdotes and so ignorant as to think that an 'easy' demonstration of the 'inadequacy' of Skinner's views about operant behaviour is to be found in an example of respondent conditioning, a mistake given added irony by the fact that it was Skinner himself who did so much to distinguish the two classes of behaviour more than 50 years ago.

In a reply to Blackman, Sutherland (1990) attempted to clarify his position:

> I am perhaps not as ignorant as he thinks: I am, for example well aware that Skinner acknowledged classical (respondent) conditioning. Indeed, I once wrote that he 'was one of the first to classify the distinction between Pavlovian conditioning and instrumental learning ... a distinction which,

as we shall see, he has since come to ignore.' It is the last phrase that is important in assessing Skinner's own theorising.

2 Most specialist textbooks (e.g. Sue, Sue & Sue, 1990) argue that approaches based on Skinnerian principles do offer a good explanation for the aetiology of at least some psychological disorders, and provide a basis for their effective treatment. Indeed, many operant conditioning techniques are embodied in several of the more cognitive approaches to therapy (e.g. Ellis, 1962; Beck, 1985). For example, some techniques to develop assertiveness or self-esteem involve practical situations of carefully graded difficulty. Mastering successful stages gives a powerful sense of control and acts as a reinforcement.

Within this talking point, students could discuss what it is that maintains *normal* behaviour. One answer could be 'probably the very same factors that are held by learning theorists to be involved in the aetiology of certain abnormal behaviours'! Behaviour modification techniques (i.e. those based on operant conditioning principles) can be viewed as re-establishing normal contingencies, and not simply a system that will fade away (or 'extinguish') outside the therapeutic setting.

Two studies that could be used in this context are those reported by Schaeffer and Martin (1969) and Lewinsohn and Libet (1972). Schaeffer and Martin describe the unintentional reinforcement of injurious head banging by nurses giving sympathy to the patients concerned. Lewinsohn and Libet propose that the absolute lack of reinforcement can be seen as the basis for depression, which might lead to 'secondary gain' as others give attention and sympathy for the depressed behaviour.

One approach to dealing with depression might be to encourage or even force the depressed person to engage in activities which are normally enjoyed. Thus, it probably is a good idea to drag a miserable friend out to do something they normally enjoy! The idea of 'secondary gain' implies that such activity should be coupled with ignoring depressed statements or behaviour. This is a little different from the normal practice of lending a sympathetic ear! Students could also discuss how far this should be taken. If, for example, a friend talked about suicide, would they pay attention (and thereby reinforce the friend's behaviour) or ignore the friend (and risk an increase in the behaviour to regain the attention which this has achieved in the past)?

3 We would argue that it seems a little unfair, and personal, for Sutherland to criticise Skinner on the basis that he and his wife suffered from phobias. Notwithstanding that point, phobias can be treated using behavioural approaches, although these are based on classical rather than operant conditioning (see Chapter 9, **Talking point 5** for a brief review of these). Skinner might have responded by claiming that he had not undergone such behaviour therapies because there was insufficient reinforcement to do so: the problems were mostly easily avoided (except when invited to climb Magdalen College tower) and may not have been that severe anyway.

Teachers could also point out that Sutherland has documented a more traumatic disorder from which he suffered (Sutherland, 1976). Using Sutherland's logic, it could be suggested that as a psychologist he should have been able to avoid the disorder or effect his own cure. This raises the question of whether we should expect psychologists to be personally superior to their fellow beings. Research quoted by Gross (1992) indicates that psychologists are not immune to the problems of their non-psychologist brethren, and are not more able than them when it comes to predicting the behaviour of others. Joynson (1974) points out that this is probably because so-called 'laypeople' are in fact already experts in practical interpersonal behaviour.

With respect to Skinner's 'unusual' applications of operant conditioning techniques, some students might ask why he wanted to investigate such a curious method of inducing urination. In Skinner's own words:

> When a parent stands by until a child urinates, before taking it back to the crib or play pen, the child may postpone urination because contact with the parent is prolonged. If, instead, the child is left alone in the toilet, it may be left much longer than is necessary and taken up with red ring around its bottom.
> (Cited in Schatzman, 1990)

Students should be able to find at least some other 'unusual' applications of operant conditioning tried by Skinner. Perhaps the most celebrated occurred during the Second World War. Skinner was enthusiastic about the possibility of exploiting the 'excellent vision' and 'extraordinary manoeuvrability' of birds, particularly pigeons and crows. Skinner believed that these birds could be used as 'devices' to guide missiles, and he built a system in which a pigeon steered by moving pairs of lightweight rods alongside its neck. Skinner discovered that if hemp seed (cannabis) was used as a reinforcer instead of grain, the pigeons were 'almost fearless'. The American military were not, however, impressed with Skinner's ideas, and as Skinner wryly noted, his 'verbal behaviour with respect to Washington underwent extinction' (Schatzman, 1990).

4 Skinner outlined a theoretical societal application of his ideas and principles of learning in *Walden Two* (1948), a novel which he completed in just seven weeks and which made him internationally famous (or infamous). Walden Pond in Massachusetts was the setting for Henry David Thoreau's account of his experiences living in a shack, and recounted in his book *Walden*. Skinner evidently discovered Walden Pond while he was at college and occasionally went swimming there.

The central character in Skinner's novel was Frazier, a self-proclaimed genius who had left psychology for behavioural engineering. Violence, jealousy, competitiveness and destructive behaviour could be eliminated by 'shaping' behaviour, with the result that all human life would be as pleasant and painless as possible. For Skinner, the citizens of Walden Two would be happy without the suffering and resentment from the repression in existing societies. In *Beyond Freedom and Dignity* (1971), another international best seller, Skinner explored these ideas further.

There has been a tendency for critics to over-simplify Skinner's approach and see it as leading to totalitarian regimes in which an individual is allowed little freedom, and control is rigid and punitive. Skinner's perspective is, in fact, very different from this. He argues that there (inevitably) already exists a high level of direction and control in society. Our supposed, and much vaunted, freedom is in fact simply allowing ourselves to be manipulated by others.

This idea has much in common with some radical sociological perspectives. For example, Gramsci (1971) talks about hegemony as the condition of being subject to normal controls by the ruling social class. As Joll (1977) notes, we accept these controls as being both normal and desirable. A similar argument has been advanced by Chomsky and Herman (1979) with respect to the influence of the media (and note that Chomsky is cited by Sutherland as a critic of Skinner!).

For Skinner, then, people are subject to social control whether they are aware of it or not. The question is not whether we allow social control, but how it will operate. Most formal social control is punitive. In Britain, for example, a greater proportion of the population is imprisoned than in any other European country. However, it could be argued that imprisonment is unsuccessful on the basis of claims made about rising crime rates. (See also Chapter 8 for a further discussion of this.)

Given that Skinner believes we should adopt positive reinforcers, and that control in our society is based on punishers or 'aversive coercion', students should be able to think of some practical ways in which Skinner's ideas could be implemented. One category of offence that could be used to discuss the issue of whether society should punish or train more desirable behaviour is child abuse.

A further topic that could be discussed here concerns those communities which have been set up in the image of Walden Two (see Masterson, 1988, for a description). Apparently, most members only stay for two or three years, but this might be because of the relatively small size of the communities and the need to integrate with the rest of society.

5 Since there are many psychologists who agree with Sutherland's claim that behaviourism is an extreme simplification of the true complexity of psychology, it is likely that there will be at least some students who hold the same view. In the article, Sutherland makes his point most forcibly:

> When a pleasurable event occurs, we interpret both the event and the responses that led to it: whether an action is repeated depends on these interpretations, which are of course determined by cognitive factors. The influence of reinforcement depends less on what a person does as what he believes he is doing ... without taking into account a person's thoughts it is impossible to know what response he is making.

Psychologists such as Heather (1976) have suggested that Sutherland's strictures also apply to the experimental approach, which is a key component of behaviourism. According to this view, carrying out experiments on behaviour is a simplistic approach which reduces a complex, interacting system to the level of isolated variables. In Sutherland's terms, 'it is as though a chemist were to try to explain the behaviour of a molecule without reference to its internal structure.'

The experimental approach could lead to a complete *misinterpretation* of the effect that variables have in combination. For example, Seligman (1975) has investigated what happens when dogs are given electric shocks and prevented from escaping them. Not only do they learn to be passive when the shocks are given, but they are highly resistant to learning that they can escape when no longer restrained. The two variables – restraint and conditioning – interact to produce a novel state of 'learned helplessness'. However, this is not capable of being predicted by the effect of either one of the variables by itself. It is, moreover, extremely important as a model for depression and as an explanation for why battered wives do not leave their husbands.

Students should appreciate that a rat's normal behaviour in the wild is much more varied than in the laboratory, and is subject to many influences (is this what Sutherland means when he talks about the Skinner box as being 'a bloodless method of decerebrating the animal'?). More recent approaches which are held to be more ecologically valid (for humans as well as rats) are largely based on observation. However, students will recognise the problems involved with this. In particular, the lack of control over variables means that it is extremely difficult to infer cause and effect relationships.

6 According to Blackman (1990), Skinner sees language as being like any other act, arising from social interaction and therefore capable of explanation in terms of its social context. Language development would make it possible to relate 'private events' from within to events which are publicly observable in the external world. For Skinner, consciousness is not an independent prior entity of which our behaviour is but a reflection, but a by-product of the 'real' processes of conditioning. Skinner did not deny cognitions, thoughts and aspirations, but saw them as outcomes of social interactions rather than as independent causes of behaviour.

Of course, 'consciousness' is a term which is very hard to pin down, and students could initially discuss what is normally meant by the term. This might include self-awareness, the continuous nature of consciousness, and a sense of self-identity. Although we all believe we possess consciousness, students could discuss whether it is in fact prevalent or necessary. Our conscious awareness is rather more fragmentary than most people think. Gilhooly (1988), for example, describes a range of very common disjointed thinking, such as daydreaming, which certainly does not involve clear awareness or consciousness.

Moreover, our conscious reasons for doing things are very often misleading. For example, research findings in social psychology are very often counterintuitive; most people believe that physical attractiveness does not greatly affect their judgement of other people, yet research shows that physical attractiveness is very important indeed (e.g. Brehm, 1992). Attribution, self-presentation, and cognitive dissonance could also be examined in this context. A case could be made for 'consciousness' being very much like Skinner's conception of it as a secondary, self-justifying process. A useful discussion of the concept of consciousness can be found in Marcel and Bisiach (1992).

With respect to the concluding remarks in his autobiography, Skinner has this to say:

> I am willing to concede that I have committed a kind of intellectual suicide in writing this autobiography ... By tracing what I have done to my environmental history rather than assigning it to a mysterious creative process, I have relinquished all chance of being called a Great Thinker. If I am right about human behaviour, I have written the autobiography of a non-person.

7 Mainstream psychology has increasingly adopted a cognitive approach to the understanding of behaviour which sees people as actively construing their environment and acting to produce anticipated outcomes. According to this approach, learning occurs as a result of a change in what we think will happen.

Thus, our internal model of the world changes as we experience it, reinforcement and punishment being two such experiences. This approach is called 'cognitive behaviourism'.

Cognitive behaviourism retains the power and much of the simplicity of conditioning as one level or type of explanation. However, it is also capable of accounting for other forms of learning which cannot be readily accounted for in a simple behaviourist model. Included here is social or observational learning, in which an individual learns from observing the outcomes of the actions of other people (e.g. Bandura, Ross & Ross, 1963).

Also included is latent learning. In this, the simple exposure to something can lead to learning without any reinforcement or punishment being given. The best known example is Tolman's (1967) demonstration of maze exploration by rats. The reason why such exploration occurs is nowadays attributed to intrinsic motivation; the task itself is the reason for doing something and does not require reinforcement or punishment. Many theorists argue that most of what we do is intrinsically motivated. Indeed, it has been shown that if reinforcement is given for something that people would do by themselves anyway, motivation is actually damaged (Lepper & Greene, 1978).

8 Species-specific learning means that some organisms are more prepared to learn certain associations than others (see, for example, Rozin, 1967; Rachlin, 1976). The work of Garcia, Ervin and Koelling (1966) shows that rats are 'primed' to associate eating or the smell/taste of food with subsequent sickness. In the wild, rats will initially only take a small sample of a new food source. If they are not adversely affected by it, they will return and eat more.

Birds, however, select food on the basis of its visual appearance rather than its smell/taste. Wilcoxin, Dragoin and Kral (1971) have demonstrated that compared with rats, quail are more easily conditioned to associate a visual stimulus with sickness. Clearly, this specialisation of learning has survival value. It is a direct challenge to the idea that associative learning is a simple and universal building block for the behaviour of all species. Further discussion of this topic can be found in Roth (1990), who gives a clear exposition of the basic theories of conditioning and the ways in which they have been modified to take account of species-specific learning and cognitive developments.

Perhaps the experience with which students will be most familiar is that of drinking too much at a party. At least some people associate either a hangover or vomiting with a particular drink. It would also be interesting for students to reflect on any subsequent habituation!

References

Bandura, A., Ross, D. and Ross, S. (1963) 'Imitation of film-mediated aggressive models', *Journal of Abnormal and Social Psychology*, 66, pp. 3–11.

Beck, A. (1985) 'Cognitive therapy, behaviour therapy, psychoanalysis, and pharmacotherapy: a cognitive continuum', **in** M. Mahoney and A. Freeman (Eds.) *Cognition and Psychotherapy*, New York: Plenum Press.

Blackman, D. (1990) 'Not a rat man but a people man', *The Guardian*, 24 August.

Brehm, S. (1992) *Intimate Relationships*, New York: McGraw Hill.

Chomsky, N. and Herman, E. (1979) *The Political Economy of Human Rights*, Nottingham: Spokesman Books.

Ellis, A. (1962) *Reason and Emotion in Psychotherapy*, New York: Stuart.

Garcia, J., Ervin, F. and Koelling, R. (1966) 'Learning with prolonged delay of reinforcement', *Psychonomic Science*, 4, pp. 123–4.

Gilhooly, K. (1988) *Thinking: Directed, Undirected and Creative*, London: Academic Press.

Gramsci, A. (1971) *Selections From The Prison Notebooks*, London: Lawrence & Wishart.

Gross, R.D. (1992) (2nd ed.) *Psychology: The Science of Mind and Behaviour*, London: Hodder & Stoughton.

Heather, N. (1976) *Radical Perspectives in Psychology*, London: Methuen.

Joll, J. (1977) *Gramsci*, London: Fontana.

Joynson, R.B. (1974) *Psychology and Common Sense*, London: Routledge.

Lepper, M. and Greene, D. (1978) *The Hidden Costs of Reward*, Hillsdale, N.J.: Lawrence Earlbaum Associates.

Lewinsohn, P. and Libet, J. (1972) 'Pleasant events, activity schedules and depression', *Journal of Abnormal Psychology*, 79, pp. 291–5.

Marcel, A.J. and Bisiach, E. (Eds.) (1992) *Consciousness in Contemporary Science*, Oxford: The Clarendon Press.

Masterson, J. (1988) 'Interview with B.F. Skinner', *The Psychologist*, 1, pp. 140–1.

Rachlin, H. (1976) *Behaviour and Learning*, San Francisco: W.H. Freeman & Co.

Roth, I. (1990) *Introduction to Psychology*, Hillsdale, N.J.: Lawrence Earlbaum Associates.

Rozin, P. (1967) 'Specific aversions as a component of specific hungers', *Journal of Comparative and Physiological Psychology*, 64, pp. 237–42.

Schaeffer, H. and Martin, P. (1969) *Behavioural Therapy*, New York: McGraw Hill.

Schatzman, M. (1990) 'Obituaries: B.F. Skinner', *The Independent*, 21 August.

Seligman, M.E.P. (1975) *Helplessness*, San Francisco: Freeman.

Skinner, B.F. (1948) *Walden Two*, New York: MacMillan.

Skinner, B.F. (1971) *Beyond Freedom and Dignity*, New York: Macmillan.

Sue, D., Sue, D. and Sue, S. (1990) *Understanding Abnormal Psychology*, Boston: Houghton Mifflin.

Sutherland, S. (1976) *Breakdown*, London: Weidenfeld & Nicolson.

Sutherland, S. (1990) 'B.F. Skinner: Behaviourism, the mind's structure, and some dinosaurs', *The Guardian*, 27 August.

Tolman, E.C. *Purposive Behaviour in Animals and Men*, New York: Irvington.

Wilcoxin, H., Dragoin, W. and Kral, P. (1971) 'Illness-induced aversions in rat and quail: relative salience of visual and gustatory cues', *Science*, 171, pp. 823–8.

6

SWITCH IN THE SHOCK TACTICS

1 There are a number of ways in which students could argue the case for and against the use of ECT as a therapeutic technique. A report by America's National Institute of Mental Health (1985) evaluated ECT using, amongst others, the following criteria:

a the type of disorder involved
b the risks of the procedure
c the implications for the administration of the therapy
d the best method for implementing the therapy

Discussion could be structured around these criteria, or around any others suggested by the teacher.

Talking points that might arise against the use of ECT include things like the side-effects of the primitive treatment methods once used (such as bruises and bone fractures), and the experience of pain due to the patient failing to lose consciousness. Memory loss could also be another argument against ECT's use, as could the claim that demonstrable brain damage has been observed in animals sacrificed immediately after ECT treatment (Breggin, 1979). It is also worth mentioning that ECT is not effective with *all* patients who undergo it.

On the positive side, it could be argued that the use of muscle relaxants overcomes (or at least minimises) the possibility of bone fractures, whilst the use of anaesthesia rules out the possibility of the patient being conscious during the treatment. Memory loss can evidently be minimised by using unilateral ECT to the non-dominant cerebral hemisphere (see below).

The fact that ECT can produce improvements in *some* severely depressed individuals, and can do so quicker than the antidepressant drugs, could also be argued to be a positive aspect of the therapy, particularly if the patient has failed to respond to other treatments. Additionally it is, as the article notes, 'impossible for patients to take an accidental or deliberate overdose of ECT'.

Students will undoubtedly have their own views over which of the factors they highlight most influences the 'cost-benefit' analysis of the therapy.

2 ECT would be particularly useful for suicidal individuals since the improvement it brings about occurs much more quickly than is the case with the antidepressant drugs. ECT would, therefore, reduce the risk that the suicidal person would harm him/herself. As the article notes, 'several hundred people die every year from suicidal antidepressant overdoses ... ECT saves quite a few lives.'

The effectiveness of ECT amongst suicidal individuals could be assessed by comparing actual suicide rates in ECT-treated individuals with those individuals treated by means of antidepressant drugs. However, students should appreciate that assessing the effectiveness of any form of therapy is an extremely difficult task. For example, it might be suggested that ECT-treated individuals could be compared with those treated by means of psychotherapy or simulated ECT (as well as those treated by psychotherapeutic drugs). As noted, in this

Talking point, Costello (1976) suggests that such approaches often fail to employ objective appraisals, that is to say, they use raters who know *exactly* what treatment each individual had received.

Students could discuss how to overcome this problem. One approach would be to use 'double blind' procedures in which raters who were *unaware* of which individual had received which treatment made assessments of the improvement that had occurred. The issue of control groups could also be made relevant here. Wessely (1993) describes a study conducted in 1965 by the Medical Research Council. This study showed that ECT was better than antidepressants or a placebo in treating depression, with 70 per cent of those receiving ECT showing a marked recovery. Unfortunately, with no control group, the study did not eliminate the possibility that ECT's effectiveness was an artefact of the elaborate procedures involved in its administration. In further studies, in which patients received either real or simulated ECT, the former was superior to the latter 'provided it was reserved only for the severest forms of depression' (Wessley, 1993).

3 There are a number of reasons why the American Psychiatric Association (APA) should have recommended ECT to be a therapy of 'last resort'. It could be argued that the APA are reacting to pressures exerted by those groups antagonistic towards ECT, or even that the Association itself is not convinced by the therapy's effectiveness. Ethical issues could be discussed here as well. Issues surrounding informed consent, freedom to withdraw, freedom to choose, and deception in 'sham' ECT could all be discussed in the context of a chronically depressed person being able to make sound judgements.

With respect to the rights of patients, at least three issues suggest themselves. One issue concerns the ward personnel making use of ECT's negative public image to induce cooperation from non-compliant patients by 'threatening' them with a series of ECT treatments. The social control of patients could also be achieved by using ECT to minimise violent and/or excited behaviour.

In support of this, Palmer (1981) cites several cases in which chronic patients on 'back wards' have experienced literally hundreds of seizures. In England, several individuals who have experienced ECT have claimed that the therapy was administered as a treatment of choice rather than as a last resort, and without any explanation of what the therapy involved. This occurred, despite the fact that the United Kingdom Central Council for Nursing's code of conduct requires that nurses should ensure that a person is fully aware of the nature, purpose and implications of any treatment before consent is given.

In Britain, the inappropriate use of ECT on children has been highlighted in the media (Independent Television, 1992). For Steve Baldwin, senior lecturer in Aberdeen University's department of Public Health, '60 children and adolescents are too many, and one child is too many ... we should not risk (ECT) on a population where the neurological system is still developing and where there is no scientific evidence to support its use. Frankly, I think that amounts to criminal assault.'

A second issue which might arise concerns a person who refuses ECT but *insists* on some other form of therapy that might not be as beneficial. The person's right to refuse treatment could be discussed by students as an issue, as could the consequent obligation of the hospital to assign one of its staff to care for that person on a 24-hour basis to ensure, for example, that s/he does not commit suicide. Some students might argue that the person should not be given special treatment: if s/he wants to commit suicide then that is his/her business. At the same time, however, it could be argued (e.g. Stone, 1975) that it cannot possibly be therapeutic for other patients to watch people kill themselves.

A third issue, which might arise, concerns the rights of other patients on the ward. If a person who had refused ECT was assigned a member of the ward staff, the other patients would be deprived of that staff member's services.

4 One way in which the 'memory loss' theory has been tested is through the use of unilateral ECT to the non-dominant cerebral hemisphere. The evidence (e.g. Abrams, Taylor, Farber, Tso, Williams & Almy, 1983) indicates that this is not only an effective method of treatment, but also results in less memory loss than either bilateral ECT or unilateral ECT to the dominant hemisphere. This finding would suggest that memory loss does not explain ECT's effectiveness.

Unfortunately, the picture is somewhat clouded by evidence reported by Rosenberg and Pettenati (1984). They showed that more treatments are necessary for unilateral ECT to achieve the same therapeutic outcome as bilateral ECT. Further confusion arises from the observation that depression itself can be associated with impaired memory loss, especially in the elderly. The article offers little support for the theory since it suggests that, for the person in question, fortnightly ECT treatment for a year produced no memory impairment 'except for the day of the treatment'.

5 In the case of von Meduna's therapy, drugs which engendered fear but did *not* produce a convulsion were shown to be ineffective in treatment. The suggestion that ECT acts as a 'punishment' which extinguishes abnormal behaviour has been tested by applying sub-convulsive shocks, that is, shocks which do not produce a convulsion. The data indicate that such treatments are ineffective. Since they are equally as unpleasant as convulsive shocks, 'punishment theory' seems unlikely to be true (Gross, 1992).

With respect to biochemical changes, it must be stressed that there are many physiological changes which occur when ECT is administered and it is difficult to establish which changes are important. However, the most likely neurotransmitters to be involved are norepinephrine and serotonin, since the role of these in the experience of endogenous depression seems to be well established (Bootzin & Acocella, 1984). It could well be that ECT influences neural transmission deep within the brain, especially in the hypothalamus and limbic system. These structures are known to be related to emotional experience. However, these is as yet little evidence to support this proposal (Carson, Butcher & Coleman, 1988).

6 It could be proposed that ECT alleviates depression by reducing rapid eye movement (REM) sleep. Clearly, this suggestion is amenable to empirical investigation and students should be able to devise an investigation to test the proposal. Additional support for the proposal could be adduced from research conducted by Scherschlicht, Polc, Schneeberger, Steiner and Haefely (1982). These researchers have shown that antidepressant drugs profoundly reduce REM sleep.

7 This **Talking point** is likely to produce lively discussion! Gross (1992) provides a summary of the main arguments. In favour of ECT, it could be argued that the lack of an accepted theory for its effectiveness shouldn't

necessarily rule out its use. Many treatment methods were either used before their mode of action were known (as in the case of citrus fruit to treat scurvy, and the use of vaccinations) or continue to be used without their precise mode of action being known (such as aspirin for relieving a headache). On the other hand, there are dangers in experimenting with the unknown. The article provides many arguments for the use of ECT, any or all of which could be argued against.

In connection with the issue of ECT-induced brain damage, the article offers evidence against Breggin's (1979) views. Cited in the article is the case of an elderly woman who had 1 250 ECTs in 28 years (an average of just under one a week). She apparently showed no evidence of brain damage. The lack of demonstrable brain damage could be linked back to **Talking point 1**, although the point should be made that not all brain damage is visible structurally.

8 A study conducted by Fink (1976) could be usefully employed here. His case-study involved a woman hospitalised for three months with severe depression. Her therapist's supervisor prescribed a course of three ECT treatments per week. What the therapist did not know was that the first 12 treatments were sub-threshold, that is, did not produce a seizure. Whilst both the therapist and the patient expected some improvement to be shown, none was observed. For the next 14 treatments, seizures were induced. After five actual seizures, both the therapist and the patient noticed a substantial improvement. This suggests that the improvement occurred as a result of the treatment and not simply from either the therapist's and/or patient's expectations.

Although students may find difficulty in identifying the variations, the nature of them is likely to elicit lively discussion. *Electronarcosis* is an intensive and prolonged form of ECT in which there is a continued passage of current over a period of up to seven minutes.

The *Glissando technique* was originally devised to reduce the severity of the muscular contractions and thereby reduce the risk of fractures. The voltage is increased rapidly (either manually or automatically) from nought to 120 volts within the period of one second. In reviewing the method, Tallett and Walker (1972) note that 'the patient may not, however, lose consciousness sufficiently rapidly and is therefore likely to be apprehensive, even resistant, to undergoing further sessions'.

The *Ectronus technique* was designed to be an improvement on the Glissando technique. It was devised by Russell (1969), and involves increasing the electric potential in steps up to 150 volts within one to two seconds. This achieves a 'relatively rapid loss of consciousness'. Russell notes that 'although some skill is required in the efficient administration of the treatment, the advantages of the method in preventing fractures, anaesthetic hazards, and the time-consuming use of anaesthetics and muscle relaxants make acquisition of this skill worthwhile' (cited in Tallett & Walker, 1972).

References

Abrams, R., Taylor, M.A., Farber, R., Tso, T.O.T., Williams, R.A. and Almy, G. (1983) 'Bilateral versus unilateral electroconvulsive therapy: efficacy in melancholia', *American Journal of Psychiatry*, 140, pp. 463–5.

Bootzin, R.R. and Acocella, J.R. (1984) *Abnormal Psychology: Current Perspectives*, New York: Random House.

Breggin, P.R. (1979) *Electroshock: Its Brain Disabling Effects*, New York: Springer Verlag.

Carson, R.C., Butcher J.N. and Coleman, J.C. (1988) *Abnormal Psychology and Everyday Life*, London: Scott, Foresman & Co.

Costello, C.G. (1976) 'Electroconvulsive therapy: Is further investigation necessary?', *Canadian Psychiatric Association Journal*, 21, pp. 61–7.

Fink, M. (1976) 'Presidential address: Brain function, verbal behaviour and psychotherapy', in R.L. Spitzer and D.F. Klein (Eds.) *Evaluation of Psychological Therapies: Psychotherapies, Behaviour Therapies, Drug Therapies and their Interactions*, Baltimore: Johns Hopkins University.

Gross, R.D. (1992) (2nd ed.) *Psychology: The Science of Mind and Behaviour*, London: Hodder & Stoughton.

Independent Television (1992) *Link*, Broadcast on 31 May and 7 June.

National Institute of Mental Health (1985) *Electroconvulsive therapy: Consensus Development Conference Statement*, Bethesda Md.: U.S. Department of Health and Human Sciences.

Palmer, R.L. (Ed.) (1981) *Electroconvulsive Therapy: An Appraisal*, New York: Oxford University Press.

Rosenberg, J. and Pettenati, H.M. (1984) 'Differential memory and unilateral ECT', *American Journal of Psychiatry*, 141, pp. 1071–4.

Russell, R.J. (1969) *Ectronus: An Improved ECT Technique*, Letchworth: Ectron.

Scherschlicht, R., Polc, P., Schneeberger, J., Steiner, M. and Haefely, W. (1982) 'Selective suppression of rapid eye movement sleep (REMS) in cats by typical and atypical antidepressants', in E. Costa and G. Racagni (Eds.) *Typical and Atypical Antidepressants: Molecular Mechanisms*, New York: Raven Press.

Stone, A.A. (1975) *Mental Health and Law: A System in Transition*, Rockville, Md.: National Institute of Mental Health.

Tallett, E.R. and Walker, K.A. (1972) *Methods of Treatment in Psychiatry*, London: Butterworths.

Wessely, S. (1993) 'Shocking treatment', *The Times*, 18 November.

7

A ROSE BY ANY OTHER NAME

1 One way in which students could examine the 'grain of truth' hypothesis is to consider the stereotypes that exist for forenames. Forenames like 'Wayne', 'Kevin', 'Sharon', and 'Tracey' are commonly stereotyped as 'having permed hair', driving a particular type of car or riding a particular type of motorcycle, drinking a certain drink in the pub, and so on. The 'grain of truth' hypothesis would be supported, at least to a degree, if students could provide examples of people with a particular forename behaving in a particular stereotypical way.

An interesting exercise related to the 'grain of truth' hypothesis involves identifying a target name and then trying to build up a stereotypical picture of the person owning the name. Once one characteristic has been identified, others will almost certainly follow. For example, a person described as driving a Citroen 2CV motor car is often perceived as voting for the Green party, wearing corduroy trousers and open-toed sandals, being vegetarian, having a beard (if male) and so on. One source of stereotypical images is *Viz* magazine, with which students will probably be familiar. This is one of the rare occasions on which the magazine can be used in a 'constructive' way!

The fact that people do make inferences corresponding with their experiences was shown by Wegner, Benel and Riley (1976). In their study, one group of participants was given a series of personality descriptions designed to cultivate certain inferences, namely that the traits of 'persuasiveness' and 'realism' were positively correlated. A second group of partici-

pants read similar descriptions, but the descriptions were designed to cultivate the inference that the traits of 'persuasiveness' and 'realism' were negatively correlated.

Afterwards, both groups were asked to read other descriptions that made no reference to 'persuasiveness' or 'realism'. However, each participant was asked to relate how 'persuasive' and 'realistic' the individual described appeared to be. The results showed that those participants given experience suggesting a positive correlation between the traits perceived a more positive correlation than the participants given experience suggesting a negative correlation. Thus, experiences can change expectancies about behaviour. Students could use this study as the basis for an investigation of the 'grain of truth' hypothesis as applied to forename stereotypes.

2 It has been suggested that illusory correlations occur because expectations about certain events distort the ways in which we process information. For example, Hamilton and Gifford (1976) asked participants to read two short statements about a variety of people. Two-thirds of the people they read about were identified as members of 'Group A'. The other one-third were identified as members of 'Group B'. Statements about the people were either 'desirable' ('John, a member of Group A (Group B), visited a sick friend in hospital') or 'undesirable' (Roy, a member of Group A (Group B), always talks about himself and his problems').

Within each group, the majority (i.e. two-thirds) were described by 'desirable' qualities. However, even though there were twice as many Group A members as Group B members, neither group had a higher *proportion* of 'desirable' or 'undesirable' members. The results indicated that although there was no real relationship between membership of either group and 'desirability', participants thought that there was, since when they read about all the people and then reported their impressions of the 'typical' member of each group, the Group B member was rated as less desirable than the Group A member.

Wegner and Vallacher (1976) have argued that the illusory correlation is similar to the fundamental attribution error. In the same way that the behaviour of other people tends to be explained in terms of personal rather than situational factors, odd behaviour can be explained by attributing it to a person's membership in an unusual group of people. When two distinctive events occur together one or more times, a person concludes that they must be causally related. According to Wegner and Vallacher, 'although [a person's] system of inference is built from his transactions with reality, in some instances his interpretations go awry. He develops expectancies and makes inferences about relationships that were never there at all'.

Moreover, once an illusory correlation is made, people tend to seek out, notice, and remember information that supports a belief. This tendency is known as the 'confirmation bias' (Baron & Byrne, 1984). As a result, the belief in non-existent correlations grows stronger. Students should recognise that illusory correlations can give rise to serious inferential errors. For example, an employer who believes that being blonde and having fun are causally linked may conclude that blondes are a poor choice for responsible jobs since they are too busy having fun (Baron & Byrne, 1984). Students could discuss the role of illusory correlation with respect to male and female forenames. An excellent discussion of the phenomenon of illusory correlation can be found in Gahagan (1991).

3 There are a number of ways in which this **Talking point** could be approached. One, but by no means the only, approach is to examine the methodology that has been used in other research concerned with stereotypes and self-fulfilling behaviour. This could be adapted to test a hypothesis about forename stereo-

typing. Two studies that could be used are described below:

a) Snyder, Tanke and Berscheid (1977): These researchers were interested in seeing if the commonly held stereotype about physically attractive people (that they are more sociable, poised, and outgoing) can be self-fulfilling. Unacquainted male and female college students were asked by the researchers to talk to each other over the telephone for about 10 minutes. Before each conversation, the man was shown a photograph of either an 'attractive' or an 'unattractive' woman, and led to believe that it was a picture of his telephone partner.

Analysis of tape recordings of the conversation showed that those who believed they were talking to an 'attractive' woman were friendly, more outgoing, and more sociable than those who believed they were talking to an 'unattractive' woman. The important finding was that judges who listened to the woman's half of the conversation, without hearing the male voice or knowing his belief about the woman's 'attractiveness', rated women whose partners believed they were 'attractive' as more sociable, poised, and humorous than women whose partners believed they were 'unattractive'. Thus, it would seem that in only 10 minutes, the men's stereotype of the physically 'attractive' women had become self-fulfilling.

b) Meichenbaum, Bowers and Ross (1969): In this study, the teachers of six girls in a class of 14 attending a school for juvenile offenders were told that the girls had high academic potential and were late developers. Observations of the teachers' behaviour revealed considerable differences towards the six girls. On later objective examinations, the girls performed significantly better than others with whom they had been matched on actual potential, classroom behaviour and the amount of attention normally received from teachers. It would seem that the teachers' expectations had influenced their behaviour towards the 'late developers', which had then influenced the performance of the girls.

4 The media clearly does play a role in the creation of stereotypical characteristics. For example, in films, the heroes typically have names like 'James' whilst villains have names like 'Boris'. Very rarely, if at all, has a world-saving hero been called 'Ernie', for instance. Similarly, certain characters on television have been very influential in producing stereotypes. Two such examples could be 'Hilda Ogden' (a character in *Coronation Street*) and 'Nora Batty' (a character in *The Last of the Summer Wine*). No doubt students will be able to generate many more examples. Some may even possess a forename which has been stereotyped as a result of a character's portrayal in a television programme.

According to Leslie Dunkling, compiler of *The Guinness Book of Names*, the name John 'is not being helped' by prominent politicians bearing it. He says, 'modern parents see John as being boring, middle-aged and lacking in character, so they are not using it.' After 1700, John was constantly among the two most popular boys names in England and Wales. However, even then it had its detractors. For example, in a letter to his sister-in-law, John Keats wrote, 'tis a bad name and goes against a man. If my name had been Edmund, I should have been more fortunate.'

According to the broadcaster and comedian John Wells,

'it is a very great relief [that John is no longer popular as a forename]. I have very clear memories of a time when I was in a studio with John Bird, the director's name was John and I think the cameraman was John as well, so it will be much easier when people are called Gawaine or Peregrine. Taxi drivers always call people John, so people on the edge of notoriety, like me, always seem more famous than we actually are.'

For boys, the top 10 names of 1993 were: 1 Daniel, 2 Matthew, 3 James, 4 Christopher, 5 Thomas, 6 Joshua, 7 Adam, 8 Michael, 9 Luke and 10 Andrew. For girls, the top 10 names were: 1 Rebecca, 2 Charlotte, 3 Laura, 4 Amy, 5 Emma, 6 Jessica, 7 Lauren, 8 Sarah, 9 Rachel and 10 Catherine.

However, the listings provided by *The Times* newspaper, which annually announces the most frequent forenames to have appeared in its Births column, differ from the most popular names among the population as a whole. In order, the most popular boys names announced in *The Times* were: Alexander, Thomas, James, William, Charles, George, Henry and Edward, Oliver and Nicholas. The 10 most popular girls names were Sophie, Olivia, Emily, Alice, Charlotte, Eleanor, Lucy, Elizabeth, Georgina and Harriet.

According to Leslie Dunkling, 'you sometimes see names high on *The Times* list which a few years later are high for the population as a whole. Parents tend to associate names with dif-

ferent classes.' Interestingly, Diana was advertised only once in *The Times* whereas Camilla (a household name after rumours surrounding Camilla Parker Bowles' relationship with the Prince of Wales) only just failed to make the top 10!

5 One way in which the hypothesis could be tested is by conceptually replicating Luchins' (1957) classic experiment. In this, participants who had been matched on measures of personality were allocated to one of four conditions. In the first, participants were presented with one paragraph describing a character called 'Jim' as 'friendly'. In the second, a single paragraph was presented which described Jim as 'unfriendly'. In the third and fourth conditions, participants were presented with both the 'friendly' and the 'unfriendly' information but in different orders. Thus, for some participants Jim was initially described as 'friendly' whilst for others he was initially described as 'unfriendly'.

When Jim was described as 'friendly' only, 95 per cent of participants rated him as friendly. When he was described as 'unfriendly' only, a mere 3 per cent of participants rated him as friendly. When Jim was first described as 'friendly' and then as 'unfriendly', 78 per cent rated him as friendly. However, when Jim was first described as 'unfriendly' and then as 'friendly', only 18 per cent rated him as friendly. Luchins termed this the *'primacy effect'*.

The primacy effect can be explained in terms of 'schematic processing' (Atkinson, Atkinson, Smith & Bem, 1993). According to this explanation, first attempts at forming impressions involve an active search in memory for the person schema or schemata that best match the incoming data. A preliminary decision that a person is 'friendly' results in discrepant information being dismissed as unrepresentative and consistent information being assimilated as representative. Support for this explanation comes from the participants in Luchins' experiment. When they were asked to account for the apparent contradictions in Jim's behaviour, it was sometimes suggested that he was 'probably tired' by the end of the day, and this explained his apparently unfriendly behaviour.

Interestingly, the primacy effect can be overcome by allowing time to elapse between the presentation of the two paragraphs. In fact, what has been termed a 'recency effect' is obtained. In this, fading memories allow more recent information to take precedence. Another way to counter the primacy effect is simply to ask participants to avoid snap judgements and weigh all the evidence before reaching a decision. A useful account of both effects can be found in Hinton (1993).

6 Whilst everyone would agree that justice should be fair and impartial in all cases and for all people, psychological research findings suggest that this is not always the case. As Baron (1989) has noted, trials and other legal proceedings are social situations which allow ample room for social factors to play a role. It has been suggested (e.g. Stewart, 1980) that members of some ethnic groups are at considerably more of a disadvantage in the courtroom than others. However, this suggestion has been challenged. For example, Welch, Gruhl and Spohn (1984) have reported that (at least as far as the United States is concerned) Blacks or other minority groups are not convicted more frequently or sentenced more harshly than Whites.

Other evidence is less equivocal about the role of social factors in decisions relating to guilt or innocence. For example, Michelini and Snodgrass (1980) have reported that 'attractive' defendants are acquitted more often than 'unattractive' defendants. Additionally, socio-economic background has been shown to bias observations about behaviour. In one study, Darley and Gross (1983) had participants watch videotapes of a child taking an academic test. Performance was rated as being 'above grade level' when the child was described as coming from a high socio-economic background and 'below grade level' when described as coming from a low socio-economic background. Other research (e.g. Goleman, 1986) has indicated that non-verbal cues given by judges can reveal their personal feelings about defendants, which then influence the verdicts given by jurors.

One study particularly worth considering by students is that reported by Stephan and Stephan (1986). They showed that in 'simulated jury studies', a male defendant's ability to speak English can affect his apparent guilt. There were three conditions in the experiment in which 'jurors' listened to tape recordings based on actual trials. In the first, a Hispanic 'defendant' spoke in accented but correct English. In the second, the 'defendant' spoke only in Spanish and his responses were translated into English. In the third condition, the 'jury' was told that while the 'defendant' could only speak Spanish, they were to disregard the fact that his

answers were being translated into English and reach their verdict only on the basis of the evidence presented.

The results showed that 'jurors' of Hispanic descent were unaffected by whether or not the 'defendant' could speak English. However, the verdicts of non-Hispanic 'jurors' were negatively affected when the 'defendant' was presented as being unable to speak English. On a 10-point rating scale of the 'defendant's' guilt, Hispanic 'jurors' (mean rating 2.92) were significantly different from non-Hispanic 'jurors' (3.77). Interestingly, in the condition in which the 'jurors' were told to disregard the 'defendant's' ability to speak English, the ratings of the Hispanic (3.29) and non-Hispanic (3.09) 'jurors' did not differ.

Thus, whilst jurors might not be unbiased, the bias *can* be removed if they are given appropriate instructions.

7 There is a large body of evidence which suggests that eye-witness testimony is not always accurate, and that memory for people is susceptible to construction. Snyder and Uranowitz's (1978) study of 'Betty K.' illustrates the *retroactive* effect of stereotypes on memory: an initially neutral description of a person, followed by certain information (e.g. heterosexual or homosexual) results in the use of a stereotype about sexuality to augment the memory of the original description. Stereotypes may also exert a *proactive effect*, in which our memory about a person is constructed from information presented and the stereotype from the information generated (Atkinson, et al. 1993). This is illustrated in the following passage taken from Hunter (1974):

> In the week beginning 23 October, I encountered in the university, a male student of very conspicuously Scandinavian appearance. I remember being very forcibly impressed by the man's nordic, Viking-like appearance – his fair hair, his blue eyes, and long bones. On several occasions, I recalled his appearance in connection with a Scandinavian correspondence I was then conducting and thought of him as the 'perfect Viking', visualising him at the helm of a long ship crossing the North Sea in quest of adventure. When I again saw the man on 23 November, I did not recognise him, and he had to introduce himself. It was not that I had forgotten what he looked like but that his appearance, as I recalled it, had become

grossly distorted. He was very different from my recollection of him. His hair was darker, his eyes less blue, his build less muscular, and he was wearing spectacles (as he always does).

As Atkinson and her colleagues have noted,

Hunter's stereotype of Scandinavians seems to have so overwhelmed any information he actually encoded about the student's appearance that the result was a highly constructed memory. It bore so little resemblance that it could not even serve as a basis for recognition.

Gross (1992) describes a number of other studies that students could use to question the accuracy of eye-witness testimony. In one (Duncan, 1976), White participants were led to believe that they were watching a live interaction between two males over closed-circuit television. When the interaction became heated, one of the participants shoved the other. The screen then went blank. Duncan manipulated the race of the interactants. In one condition they were two White men and in another two Black men. In a third condition a White man shoved a Black man, and in a fourth a Black man shoved a White man. Participants were asked to classify the behaviour as 'playing around', 'dramatising', 'aggressiveness' or 'violence'. The results showed that the participants classified the Black man's shove as 'violence', especially if he shoved a White man.

Other studies (e.g. Rothbart, Evans & Fulero, 1979; Howard & Rothbart, 1980) have shown that people are better able to recall those facts which support their stereotypes, and that there is a tendency to have better recall of facts which are critical of the minority than facts which are favourable.

One area in which similar processes have been shown to operate is applications for courses. In a study conducted by Linville and Jones (1980), participants were given written descriptions of applications to law school. When the applicant was described as being particularly poor, those applicants described as Black were judged more negatively than those described as White. Presumably, the Black applicant was seen as being more 'typical' and, therefore, more unimpressive. However, when the applicant was described as being particularly impressive, Black applicants were judged far more positively than White applicants, presumably because the Black applicant was seen as being more exceptional and therefore all the more impressive. Students should be able to think of other areas in which a similar bias might operate.

References

Atkinson, R.L., Atkinson, R.C., Smith, E.E. and Bem, D.J. (1993) *Introduction to Psychology*, London: Harcourt Brace Jovanovich.

Baron, R.A. (1989) *Psychology: The Essential Science*, London: Allyn & Bacon.

Baron, R.A. and Byrne, D.S. (1984) *Social Psychology: Understanding Human Interaction*, London: Allyn & Bacon.

Darley, J.M. and Gross, P.H. (1983) 'A hypothesis-confirming bias in labelling effects', *Journal of Personality and Social Psychology*, 44, pp. 20–33.

Duncan, S.L. (1976) 'Differential social perception and attribution of intergroup violence: testing the lower limits of stereotyping of Blacks', *Journal of Personality and Social Psychology*, 34, pp. 590–8.

Gahagan, J. (1991) 'Understanding other people; understanding self', in J. Radford and E. Govier (Eds.) *A Textbook of Psychology*, London: Routledge.

Goleman, D. (1986) 'Studies point to the power of nonverbal signals', *The New York Times*, 8 April, C1-C6.

Gross, R.D. (1992) (2nd ed.) *Psychology: The Science of Mind and Behaviour*, London: Hodder & Stoughton.

Hamilton, D.L. and Gifford, R.K. (1976) 'Illusory correlation in interpersonal perception: a cognitive basis of stereotypic judgements', *Journal of Experimental Social Psychology*, 12, pp. 392–407.

Hinton, P.R. (1993) *The Psychology of Interpersonal Perception*, London: Routledge.

Howard, J.W. and Rothbart, M. (1980) 'Social categorization and memory for ingroup and outgroup behaviour', *Journal of Personality and Social Psychology*, 38, pp. 301–10.

Hunter, I.M.L. (1974) *Memory*, Harmondsworth: Penguin.

Linville, P.W. and Jones, E.E. (1980) 'Polarised appraisals of outgroup members', *Journal of Personality and Social Psychology*, 38, pp. 689–703.

Luchins, A. (1957) 'Primacy-recency in impression formation', **in** C.I. Hovland (Ed.) *The Order of Presentation in Persuasion*, New Haven: Yale University Press.

Meichenbaum, D.H., Bowers, K.S. and Ross, R.R. (1969) 'A behavioural analysis of teacher expectancy effects', *Journal of Personality and Social Psychology*, 13, pp. 306–16.

Michelini, R.L. and Snodgrass, S.R. (1980) 'Defendant characteristics and juridic decisions', *Journal of Research in Personality*, 14, pp. 340–50.

Rothbart, M., Evans, M. and Fulero, S. (1979) 'Recall for confirming events: memory processes and the maintenance of social stereotyping', *Journal of Experimental Social Psychology*, 15, pp. 343–55.

Snyder, M., Tanke, E.D. and Berscheid, E. (1977) 'Social perception and interpersonal behaviour: on the self-fulfilling nature of social stereotypes', *Journal of Personality and Social Psychology*, 35, pp. 656–66.

Snyder, M. and Uranowitz, S.W. (1978) 'Reconstructing the past: some cognitive consequences of person perception', *Journal of Personality and Social Psychology*, 36, pp. 941–50.

Stephan, C.W. and Stephan, W.G. (1986) 'Habla Ingles? The effects of language translation on simulated juror decisions', *Journal of Applied Social Psychology*, 16, pp. 577–89.

Stewart, J.E. (1980) 'Defendant's attractiveness as a factor in the outcome of criminal trials: an observational study', *Journal of Applied Social Psychology*, 10, pp. 348–61.

Wegner, D.M. and Vallacher, R.R. (1976) *Implicit Psychology: An Introduction to Social Cognition*, New York: Oxford University Press.

Wegner, D.M., Benel, D.C. and Riley, E.N. (1976) 'Changes in perceived inter-trait correlations as a function of experience with persons', *Paper presented at the meeting of the Southwestern Psychological Association*, Alberquerque (April).

Welch, S., Gruhl, J. and Spohn, C. (1984) 'Dismissal, conviction, and incarceration of Hispanic defendants: a comparison with Anglos and Blacks', *Social Science Quarterly*, pp. 257–64.

8

HOW BRITAIN LOST ITS CONSCIENCE

1 Some students may already have studied philosophy and should be readily able to attack Lynn's rather crude and populist formulation of morality. The important point that all students should appreciate, however, is that common-sense approaches (like Lynn's) quickly fall down when applied to more complex social issues. Students could consider drug taking among young people. Whilst up to 50 per cent of young people take illegal drugs at some time (Johnston, O'Malley & Bachman, 1992), very few go on to become addicted. Thus, whilst illegal drug taking is at a high level it does not (arguably) result in major social problems. Although some people develop an addiction, this may be a means of expressing an underlying problem rather than being the problem itself.

If the concern really is with the safety or stability of society, then it is an interesting question as to why many acceptable, but damaging, activities are not labelled as deviant. Students with a knowledge of sociology might quickly generate ideas about the economic interests involved. An accessible introduction to this area, which could be used for further discussion of this issue, can be found in Holdaway (1988).

2 As Lynn suggests, the concept of punishment is 'unfashionable. It raises liberal hackles.' However, whilst there may be 'scientific reasons to believe that discipline and punishment can modify behaviour', as Lynn suggests, there are also good psychological reasons why incarceration in prison is an ineffec-

tive way of deterring criminal activity. These include the low probability of being caught (and punished), the long delay between the act and the punishment, and the fact that punishment (imprisonment) does not teach new, positive behaviours.

The evidence suggests that the low probability of being caught means that most criminals hardly think about incarceration at all when contemplating and committing crimes (e.g. Giddens, 1993). Students will, however, probably baulk at the suggestion that *nothing* be done to those who engage in criminal activity. It would be interesting to discover why students would find it hard to 'let people get away with it'.

An alternative to punishment suggests that deviant behaviours should be subject to some form of treatment, the intention being to develop a less deviant way of life. A behaviourist approach would emphasise a regime that reinforces alternative and more appropriate behaviours. This might include social skills training and/or training in vocational abilities which could be used to gain employment. It could be argued that this would best be done in the community rather than in the false social context of a prison. Indeed, there are such things as 'Intermediate Treatment' schemes. These are local alternatives to custodial care, such as community service projects. The implementation of these has dramatically reduced the use of custodial sentences for juvenile offenders. Indeed, some Intermediate Treatment schemes have actually reduced local crime rates among juvenile offenders.

3 It may be difficult for students to recall a specific example or examples and they may need some prompting. This might involve asking whether they can recall a situation in which they did not know how to behave and took their cue from a parent (such as the first time at a barber's or a hairdresser's). An alternative approach would be to ask whether any student was ever upset by an unusual transgression on the part of the mother or father. Such a response would indicate that the individual had taken on the normal social values of the parent(s). If students cannot recall any transgression, they could be asked how they *would* feel in such circumstances. An example might be if they were to witness one of their parents shoplifting.

There are several examples that could be used to illustrate the modelling of positive social behaviour by parents. One would be the parent driving a car in a careful and non-aggressive way. Hopefully, the benefits are that the journey is both much safer and non-stressful. Students should be able to generate other examples.

4 The issue of physical punishment is certain to generate a great deal of controversy and discussion. The administration of physical punishment by parents is actually banned in many European countries (such as Sweden). Whilst it is prevalent in Britain, its use is currently the subject of much controversy. Leach (1993) has published a useful and easily obtainable article which could be used as a basis for discussion. Students could also recount their own experiences of physical punishment, and their feelings at the time. They might be asked, for example, whether they had any sense of the punishment leading to more positive behaviours.

According to Leach (1993), the evidence generally indicates that children who are physically punished are much more likely to use physical punishment when they become parents themselves. This is presumably because they have not learned any other effective techniques that can be used when their own children's behaviour becomes a problem. Alternative techniques that could be discussed include positive reinforcement (the rewarding of good behaviour), negative reinforcement (the removal of reinforcers which are then given back when the desired behaviour occurs), and counselling strategies (talking through the situation and the consequences). Discussion could be promoted through the use of hypothetical problem situations. An example would be one child behaving aggressively towards another.

The case of Anne Davis could also be used as the basis for discussion. In July 1993, Davis appealed against Sutton Borough Council's decision to remove her from its register of childminders for refusing to undertake not to smack children in her care. Council policy insists that childminders must promise not to use corporal punishment and cites the Department of Health guidance published with the 1989 Children Act.

Professor Lynn spoke in support of Davis' appeal, suggesting that 'for some children, physical discipline is an important part of that [i.e. morality] process. From time to time the most effective way of controlling a child is a light smack.' Lynn informed the court that 'children whose parents and minders did not use any physical punishment were less likely to learn what behaviour was "socially acceptable".' Davis was given further support by another 'expert witness', Lynn Burrows, a writer on child care who claimed that 'young children particularly understand a smack better than verbal reasoning and were happier with it.' Miss Anne Foreman, the mother of one of the children minded by Davis, agreed that Davis should be allowed to smack her child when she felt it necessary: 'I believe that if a child is disciplined well in the early years he makes a good adult', she said.

Sutton magistrates subsequently ruled in Davis' favour: 'there is nothing to prevent a parent using lawful chastisement on their child and this includes appropriate smacking. Therefore a parent must have the right to arrange with another to use this. The chosen person can be a childminder.' However, according to Allan Levy, QC, who investigated the 'pindown' regime in Staffordshire children's homes, 'there is a strong argument that now we've ratified the United Nations Convention on the Rights of the Child, article nine imposes on the Government a duty to prevent any kind of punishment.' In March 1994, the High Court ruled that the magistrates were within their rights to overturn Sutton Borough Council's decision not to register Davis as a child-minder. No doubt there will be other cases like this in the future.

5 According to Lynn,

'high levels of crime, drugs, promiscuity and chronic unemployment have become characteristic of inner-city communities. These characteristics are passed from one generation to another by parents [which] may explain the decline in moral values in so many parts of Europe and America. Parents suffer little or no social disgrace if their children turn out badly.'

Although the evidence (*Social Trends*, 1993) indicates that children from single-parent families are generally more likely to be in trouble with the law, this certainly does not seem to be due to an inevitable lack of morality. A number of writers (e.g. Cochrane, 1993) argue that the critical driving factor is the level of economic stress that the single parent family is under. It therefore seems probable that applying economic sanctions to such families will eventually result in *even more* problems.

6 Students will hopefully realise that explanations of social behaviour are most effective when they are based on an understanding of social psychological and sociological concepts. Lynn does not really look at these, and it could be suggested that he is guilty of oversimplifying what is an already complex issue.

A major alternative to seeing deviance as mainly based on moral problems within the family has been proposed by writers such as Cloward and Ohlin (1960). The argument is that high levels of unemployment and increasing differences between the rich and poor lead to a sense of exclusion for those sectors of society whose members are unable to achieve economic or social success. They therefore establish subcultures whose roles and norms are very different from the rest of society, and are often actually opposed to it. Membership of, and identification with, these subcultures therefore becomes the moral context for individuals. Although this perspective is essentially sociological, it requires a pyschological understanding of the processes of social influence such as conformity.

One answer to the question of why Lynn does not adopt the above approach might just be that he is not aware of it. An alternative, and more plausible suggestion, however, is that the 'rightist' beliefs are politically popular and appear to offer a simple solution to pressing problems. The alternatives of reducing inequality and giving people legitimate common values is a much more difficult prospect, since it would involve profound changes in present-day society and would be hugely threatening to a complex web of interests. Foucault (1971) writes persuasively of the ways in which scientific concepts and technology are social constructs determined by the needs of society and which maintain social control.

7 As noted in the **Background**, Kohlberg (1976) based his theory of moral development on Piaget's theory of cognitive development. For Kohlberg, moral development meets the requirements of a 'stage theory' since the stages are held to be qualitatively different yet logically related. Within a given stage, thinking shows some consistency (Benjamin, Hopkins & Nation, 1987).

Like Piaget, Kohlberg used the 'clinical method' in which people were asked to make moral decisions based on verbal descriptions of moral dilemmas. These included the commitment involved in a promise and a mercy killing, and the value of human life. Kohlberg also asked his respondents to answer follow-up questions. On the basis of the responses supplied, Kohlberg was able to classify moral development into three levels and six stages (see below). Longitudinal projects (e.g. Colby, Kohlberg, Gibbs & Lieberman, 1983) have tended to support Kohlberg's views, and it has been claimed that morality does develop towards higher stages in a fixed sequence (Snarey, Reimer & Kohlberg, 1985).

Lynn mentions one of the dilemmas reported in Kohlberg (1976). Students might be interested in the full version used by Kohlberg (1976):

In Europe, a woman was near death from a special kind of cancer. There was one drug that the doctors thought might save her. It was a form of radium that a druggist in the same town had recently discovered. The drug was expensive to make, but the druggist was charging 10 times what the drug cost him to make. He paid $200 for the radium and charged $2000 for a small dose of the drug. The sick woman's husband, Heinz, went to everyone he knew to borrow the money, but could only get together about $1000, which was half of what it cost. He told the druggist that his wife was dying and asked him to sell it cheaper or let him pay later. But the druggist said, 'No, I discovered the drug and I'm going to make money from it.' So Heinz got desperate and broke into the man's store to steal the drug for his wife.

Kohlberg was not particularly interested in

whether respondents thought the husband should steal the drug, since such a judgement depends too much on a person's religious or ethical upbringing. Instead, Kohlberg examined the *way* each respondent came to a decision and the factors involved in making a choice. The results led Kohlberg to distinguish between three levels of reasoning that boys seem to progress through as they grow older. Each level consists of two separate stages, giving a total of six stages in the development of moral reasoning. As noted above, Kohlberg suggests that these always appear in the same order, though not everyone goes through all six:

THE PRE-CONVENTIONAL LEVEL

Stage One – Punishment and Obedience Orientation
Characteristics – Obeys rules to avoid punishment

Stage Two – Market-place Orientation
Characteristics – Seeks rewards, or having favours returned

THE CONVENTIONAL LEVEL

Stage Three – Good-boy Orientation
Characteristics – Conforms to avoid disapproval by others

Stage Four – Law and Order Orientation
Characteristics – Conforms to avoid blame by legitimate authorities

THE POST-CONVENTIONAL LEVEL

Stage Five – Social Contract, Legalistic Orientation
Characteristics – Obeys rules for approval by others concerned with the welfare of the community

Stage Six – Universal Ethical Principle Orientation
Characteristics – Acts on basis of own ethical principles, freely chosen

There is evidence to suggest that in different cultures, moral judgements evolve through the stage sequences suggested by Kohlberg (e.g. Snarey, 1985). However, there is some debate over whether the stages are as *fixed* as Kohlberg suggests (e.g. Kurtines & Greif, 1974). Students should also be aware of research linking moral reasoning to delinquency, honesty, altruism, and other types of moral behaviour

(e.g. Blasi, 1980). The relationships are often complex, and the evidence suggests that the fact that people know something is right does not necessarily mean they will do it.

Hassett (1981), for example, asked adults to predict their behaviour in a number of everyday ethical dilemmas (such as returning extra change to a grocery clerk). In many cases people said that keeping the change would be wrong, but they would do it anyway. On other ethical dilemmas of this sort, Hassett found that two out of three respondents predicted that they would act in a way they themselves considered wrong. This raises the interesting question of what *conditions* are necessary for people to choose a course of action they consider wrong. Students could discuss this point further.

One important criticism of Kohlberg's research is the fact that the stages are based solely on the study of boys and men. According to Carol Gilligan (1982), Kohlberg's stages are thus based on a male definition of morality. When women were studied, Gilligan reported that they reached the higher stages of moral development less frequently than men. Gilligan asserts that men and women have different concepts of morality, such that men apply abstract ethics and universal principles to make decisions on moral issues, whereas women make moral judgements according to a more personal standard which takes into consideration interpersonal relationships and responsibilities to other people (e.g. Kurdek & Krile, 1982). Students could discuss Gilligan's claim that, 'the very traits that traditionally have defined the "goodness" of women, their care for and sensitivity to the needs of others, are those that mark them as deficient in moral development'. Recent research investigating this issue is reported in Clopton & Sorell (1993).

With respect to the issue of moral progress, Bee (1992) gives a good review of the various theories of moral development and the effectiveness of various attempts to encourage progress. One approach is to set up discussion groups and expose children to the moral reasoning of other people. This seems to be particularly effective when focused on moral dilemmas, and can lift moral reasoning by half a stage (Schaefli, Rest & Rhomas, 1985). An even more effective approach is to incorporate real-life moral decisions into such groups. These have involved giving students collective responsibility for, amongst other things, deciding on school rules. In one school where this was carried out, low level crime virtually disappeared! Other processes are probably at work here, including social influence. One could, perhaps, use this as the establishment of a non-deviant subculture.

References

Bee, H. (1992) *The Developing Child*, London: Harper Collins.

Benjamin, L.T., Hopkins, J.R. and Nation, J.R. (1987) *Psychology*, New York: MacMillan.

Blasi, A. (1980) 'Bridging moral cognition and moral action: a critical review of the literature', *Psychological Bulletin*, 88, pp. 1–45.

Clopton, N.A. and Sorell, G.T. (1993) 'Gender differences in moral reasoning. Stable or situation?', *Psychology of Women Quarterly*, 17, pp. 85–101.

Cloward, R. and Ohlin, L. (1960) *Delinquence and Opportunity*, New York: Free Press.

Cochrane, A. (1993) 'The problems of poverty', **in** R. Dallos and E. McLaughlin (Eds.) *Social Problems and the Family*, London: Sage Publications.

Colby, A., Kohlberg, L., Gibbs, J. and Lieberman, M.A. (1983) 'Longitudinal study of moral judgement', *Monographs of the Society for Research in Child Development*, 48, (1, Serial No. 200).

Foucault, M. (1971) *Madness and Civilisation: A History of Insanity in the Age of Reason*, London: Tavistock.

Giddens, A. (1993) *Sociology*, Cambridge: Polity Press.

Gilligan, C. (1982) *In a Different Voice: Psychological Theory and Women's Development*, Cambridge, MA: Harvard University Press.

Hassett, J. (1981) 'But that would be wrong', *Psychology Today*, November, pp. 34–50.

Holdaway, S. (1988) *Crime and Deviance*, London: MacMillan.

Johnston, L., O'Malley, P. and Bachman, J. (1992) *Illicit Drug Use, Smoking, and Drinking by America's High School Students, College Students, and Young Adults, 1975–1991*, Rockville, MD: National Institute on Drug Abuse DHHS Publication Nos. (ADM) 92-1920 and (ADM) 92-1940.

Kohlberg, L. (1976) 'Moral stages and moralisation: Cognitive-developmental approach', **in** T. Likona (Ed.) *Moral Development and Behaviour: Theory, Research and Social Issues*, New York: Holt, Reinhart & Winston.

Kurdek, L.A. and Krile, D. (1982) 'A developmental analysis of the relation between peer acceptance and both interpersonal understanding and perceived social competence', *Child Development*, 53, pp. 1491–95.

Kurtines, W. and Greif, E.B. (1974) 'The development of moral thought: review and evaluation of Kohlberg's approach', *Psychological Bulletin*, 81, pp. 453–70.

Leach, M.P. (1993) 'Should parents hit their children?', *The Psychologist*, 6, pp. 216–20.

Schaefli, A., Rest, J. and Rhomas, S. (1985) 'Does moral education improve moral judgement? A meta-analysis of intervention studies using the Defining Issues Test', *Review of Educational Research*, 55, pp. 319–52.

Snarey, J.R. (1985) 'Cross-cultural universality of social-moral development: a critical review of Kohlbergian research', *Psychological Bulletin*, 97, pp. 202–32.

Snarey, J.R., Reime, J. and Kohlberg, L. (1985) 'Development of social-moral reasoning among Kibbutz adolescents: a longitudinal cross-cultural study', *Developmental Psychology*, 21, pp. 3-17.

9

GRIT YOUR TEETH AND ENJOY IT

1 Using questionnaires or conducting interviews is, as most students will probably be aware, fraught with difficulties. According to Lindsay and Jackson (1993), 'it is difficult to determine the intensity of fear reported by respondents because the questions ... provide no anchors for the description of anxiety.' In the Dutch study conducted by Schuurs, Duivenvoorden, van Velzen and Verhage (1981), for example, respondents were asked if they 'generally' **a)** 'were afraid of dental treatment' and **b)** 'dread(ed) dental visits'. For the second question, respondents were instructed to answer 'Yes', 'No', 'Somewhat' or 'Does not apply'. Lindsay and Jackson argue that because the question asks about a *private event*, it would be impossible for observers to tell if one group of respondents who acknowledged a 'dread' of dentistry experienced more fear than another group of respondents who denied experiencing the same dread.

Other surveys have used the Dental Anxiety Scale (DAS) devised by Corah (1969). Amongst other things, this asks respondents 'waiting in the dentist's office' if they are 'relaxed', 'a little uneasy', 'tense', 'anxious' or 'so anxious that [they] sometimes break out in a sweat or feel almost physically sick'. Even with this slightly more sophisticated scale, however, it has been shown that respondents differ in the their perception of physiological changes as depicted in the DAS, and that such changes do not correlate highly with a respondent's description of the intensity of his/her fear. For example, a respondent describing him/herself as 'very afraid' may not perceive or show a correspondingly high pulse rate (Nietzel, Bernstein & Russell, 1988).

With respect to Christine Higgs, the article suggests that even hearing the word 'dentist' would have made her 'crawl up the wall'. Students should be able to identify the most revealing passage in the article as that which says, 'she heard a dentist's drill while listening to a tape at work. She started hyperventilating and said she could not complete the typing. It took her 24 hours to recover her emotional equilibrium.' Perhaps a more straightforward behavioural assessment of dental anxiety is how often an individual attends the dentist's. This point is discussed in detail below.

2 A study conducted by Wardle (1982) indicated that women reported experiencing more fear than men concerning dental procedures, a finding consistent with other studies in this area and with the well-established sex differences in anxiety. One potential answer to this question is that women are more concerned than men with their facial appearance, and this concern outweighs the fear of attending. More generally, it has been found that some people who are terrified of dentistry will attend because they believe in the prophylactic value of dental treatment; it prevents them from developing a serious dental disease which might require an even more terrifying form of intervention.

As far as exercising caution when 'frequency of attendance' is used as a measure of the intensity of fear, Lindsay and Woolgrove (1989) have noted that almost all surveys asking respondents how often they visit the dentist's have relied on self-report indications of attendance. Eddie (1984) has suggested that such reports *overestimate* the frequency of attendance. In Eddie's study, 39 per cent of respondents claimed to attend 'frequently' but dental records indicated that this was in fact true for only 16 per cent.

3 The article suggests that Christine 'cannot identify the exact moment her problem began'. However, it does note that 'during the seventies she had dental treatment a couple of times, but only with the help of intravenously administered sedatives. The first knocked her out, but she came round during the second.' It could be suggested that Christine experienced pain when she awoke, and that this led to the development of her fear. Alternatively, Christine may have had a painful experience prior to her treatment during the seventies, since routine dental treatment is *not* ordinarily carried out using intravenously administered sedatives.

The article suggests several other experiences that may lead to an association forming between visiting the dentist's and the expectation of pain. For example, one patient 'had been slapped by her previous dentist and told not to be so stupid'. Additionally, the article describes a man who 'had a fear of injections after having a cholera shot while abroad. The needles used were so old and blunt that it took four attempts to complete the injection.' Students could discuss this as evidence for the generalisation of fear from one situation to another. It is also worth noting that dentists have reported that local anaesthetics can fail to protect patients from pain (Kuster & Rakes, 1987). This supports Melamed's (1979) view that the anxiety aroused by dentistry is different from other clinical anxieties because there actually is the possibility of experiencing discomfort at the dentist's.

According to Lindsay and Jackson (1993), procedures for identifying the causes of dental fear have typically used interviews or questionnaires. As they note:

> Unfortunately, the validity of retrospective assessment of dental histories, thus assessed, is rarely challenged. However, Kent (1985) has concluded that recall of dental treatment can change to be consistent with the level of fear associated with dentistry. This suggests that the process of recalling a dental history may not be independent of the patient's

perceptions of their being afraid of dentistry. Events may be described as distressing by patients in order to account for their dental fear.

In those studies in which dental histories are obtained from a source more independent of the person concerned (such as parents in the case of children), the evidence suggests that not all have had an experience at the dentist's which is sufficient to account for the high level of fear reported (Sermet, 1974). According to Davey (1989), people who have had a painful experience at the dentist's may not develop a fear of dentistry because they have previously been exposed to dental treatment in a benign way, protecting them from subsequent distressing experiences relating to dentistry. It has been shown, for example, that people who have experienced dental treatment can be *less* fearful than people without that experience (Murray, Liddell & Donohue, 1989).

4 Studies should be able to suggest some factors that could contribute to a fear of dentistry. In his original study, Lautch (1971) identified a proportion of nervous dental patients who had, on average, higher levels of neuroticism. Other research (e.g. Liddell, 1990) has indicated that at least some nervous dental patients have a higher level of general anxiety, or a greater number of other fears, than non-frightened dental patients. However, as Lindsay and Jackson (1993) have remarked,

> While this research indicates that highly nervous dental patients often have many other fears, [it] does not show why these patients have certain fears, including dental fear, and not others ... In addition, it has not been shown that all neurotic [patients] are highly afraid of dentistry.

Causal relationships between variables can, of course, be assessed by means of an experiment. Students should be encouraged to think carefully about the design of an experiment to establish a causal link, and particularly encouraged to consider the ethical questions such an experiment would be likely to raise.

5 Students could be either introduced to, or reminded about, the various behaviour therapies. Briefly, the main therapies are:

a *Stimulus Satiation*: the presentation of a desired stimulus until the desire or motivation for that stimulus no longer exists.

b *Covert Sensitisation*: a method for extinguishing undesirable behaviour by associating unpleasant mental images with that behaviour.

c *Aversion Therapy*: the use of punishment or aversive stimulation to eliminate an undesirable behaviour.

d *Flooding*: confrontation of the anxiety producing stimulus in an attempt to eliminate, through extinction, the anxiety experienced.

e *Systematic/Imaginal Systematic Desensitisation*: the simultaneous use of relaxation techniques and imagined to real contact with the anxiety arousing stimulus. A hierarchy of feared contacts is established. The patient and therapist work through the hierarchy, the therapist's main role being to prevent the anxiety response from being elicited.

Students should recognise that some of the above techniques are more appropriate to the treatment of fear of dentistry than others! It would be interesting to see if students can devise an appropriate therapeutic schedule and also consider the ethical issues their chosen therapy might involve. From the description given in the article, it could be suggested that Dr Lindsay is using a desensitisation procedure which might be termed *'Reciprocal Inhibition Therapy'*. In this, a new response which is incompatible with the response to be eliminated is conditioned. Anxiety and relaxation are incompatible responses, and the former can be removed by conditioning the latter response to a stimulus that previously evoked it.

Students could also discuss the 'stimulus substitution hypothesis' in this connection. According to this hypothesis, if the behavioural manifestations alone of a disorder are treated, the 'conflict' (in psychodynamic terms) which caused the disorder in the first place will emerge elsewhere (and may do so in a potentially more serious form). Behaviour therapy only deals with the maladaptive behaviour and does not address underlying 'conflicts'.

Other psychological techniques that have been used to treat dental fear include *video modelling*, *coping rehearsal*, and *hypnosis*. The article suggests that hypnosis can be successful and it has certainly been used widely by dentists as a treatment for fear (Milgrom, Weinstein, Kleinknecht & Getz, 1985). However, students should be aware that the empirical evidence actually suggests that hypnosis is no more effective than no treatment at all (McAmmond, Davidson & Kovitz, 1971).

Coping rehearsal is based on the idea that if it is known that an unusually stressful situation is about to occur, then it should be possible to 'inoculate' the individual by providing information about it ahead of time, and suggesting ways of dealing with it. This idea is discussed further in **7** below. Video modelling has been used to encourage non-attenders to volunteer for dental treatment. The technique involves those fearful of dentistry being shown a video of patients undergoing dental treatment successfully. There is some evidence that the method can be successful (Lindsay & Busch, 1981).

6 The article suggests that 'nervous parents may transmit their fears to their children.' This can be achieved in a number of ways, including the modelling of dental fear to children by parents or others, or by children hearing reports of distressing dental treatment. In adults, it has been shown that the severity of pain which is expected to be experienced is significantly more than that actually experienced (Kent, 1985). Several studies (e.g. Huq, Lindsay & Roberts, 1992) have shown that similar unrealistic expectations of discomfort occur in children. Since the available evidence suggests that once the expectation of pain is established it is very difficult to change, the most obvious way to tackle a child's fear would be more consistent modelling of dental treatment free from stress, especially by mothers (Lindsay, 1984).

As far as the dentist is concerned, Fenwick, Busch and Lindsay (1980) reported that in 40 'very nervous' children, over half attributed their fear to an unpleasant experience during dental treatment (such as restraint of the child by the dentist). As Lindsay and Woolgrove (1982) have noted, 'either the dentist's method of management contributed to this, or his/her management was ineffective in limiting the distress suffered during uncomfortable treatment.' Approaches which have been shown to be effective include providing information about the sensations of treatment, rewarding appropriate behaviour, and giving some control over treatment (Thrash, Marr & Box, 1982). The role of control is discussed in **7** below.

7 Laboratory studies of pain stimulation of teeth indicate that increases in anxiety raise sensitivity to pain. Clearly, then, there are good reasons for dentists to employ strategies to minimise the amount of anxiety experienced. According to Jackson (1992), 65 per cent of dental patients would prefer to have information about pain management, and over 80 per cent would want to know how to control the progress of treatment with 'stop signals'.

Lindsay and Jackson (1990) devised a leaflet which advised adult patients new to a dental practice that the dentist would tell them about pain management. Lindsay and Jackson reported a significant reduction in anxiety amongst the 'most nervous' patients who were given the leaflet. The advantages of leaflets are that their contents can be checked for ease of understanding, they can be given to patients by receptionists at any time before treatment, and the information may be remembered more easily than verbally delivered information (Lindsay & Jackson, 1993).

Students should note that, at least with adults, providing information about the *sensations* to be experienced during and after surgical procedures does not appear to be either effective or appropriate in dentistry (Lindsay, Wege & Yates, 1984). Lindsay and his colleagues suggest that whilst patients are nervous if they are uncertain about the sensations to be experienced, most are able to predict accurately the nature of the sensations likely to be produced.

8 Students may suggest a variety of explanations for the demographic differences. These might be based on their political beliefs or stereotypical beliefs about 'Northerners' and 'Southerners'. Whilst lively discussion of this point is likely, students should be reminded that simple single factor explanations are unlikely to be true. It is much more likely that a multiplicity of variables interact to give rise to the observed differences.

9 Reber (1985) uses the word 'odontophobia' to describe a) fear of teeth, and b) fear of having one's teeth worked on by a dentist. Strictly speaking, only a) is correct. We would suggest that b) is better described by the word *odontoiatrophobia* or 'fear of the tooth doctor'.

References

Corah, N.L. (1969) 'Development of a dental anxiety scale', *Journal of Dental Research*, 48, p. 596.

Davey, G.C.L. (1989) 'Dental phobias and anxieties: evidence for conditioning processes in the acquisition and modulation of a learned fear', *Behaviour Research and Therapy*, 27, pp. 51–8.

Eddie, S. (1984) 'Frequency of attendance in the General Dental Service in Scotland: a comparison with claimed attendance', *British Dental Journal*, 157, pp. 267–70.

Fenwick, J., Busch, C.J. and Lindsay, S.J.E. (1980) 'Helping the nervous patient: the presence of the parent and other procedures', *Annual Conference of the British Paedodontic Society*.

Huq, A., Lindsay, S.J.E. and Roberts, J. (1992) 'Children's expectations and recollections of discomfort associated with dental treatment', *International Journal of Paediatric Dentistry*, 2, pp. 11–16.

Jackson, C.P. (1992) 'Preferences for, and effects of, preparatory information in dental patients', *unpublished Ph.D. thesis, Institute of Psychiatry*, University of London.

Kent, G. (1985) 'Memory of dental pain', *Pain*, 21, pp. 187–94.

Kuster, G.C. and Rakes, G. (1987) 'Frequency of inadequate local anaesthesia in child patients', *Journal of Paediatric Dentistry*, 3, pp. 7–9.

Lautch, H. (1971) 'Dental phobia', *British Journal of Psychiatry*, 119, pp. 151–8.

Liddell, A. (1990) 'Personality characteristics versus medical and dental experiences of dentally anxious children', *Journal of Behavioural Medicine*, 13, pp. 183–94.

Lindsay, S.J.E. (1984) 'The fear of dental treatment: a critical and theoretical analysis', **in** S. Rachman (Ed.) *Contributions to Medical Psychology III*, Oxford: Pergamon Press.

Lindsay, S.J.E. and Busch, C.J. (1981) 'Behaviour modification in dentistry: a review', *Behavioural Psychotherapy*, 9, pp. 200–14.

Lindsay, S.J.E. and Jackson, C. (1990) **Cited in** Lindsay and Jackson (1993).

Lindsay, S.J.E. and Jackson, C. (1993) 'Fear of routine dental treatment in adults: its nature and management', *Psychology and Health*, 8, pp. 135–53.

Lindsay, S.J.E. and Woolgrove, J. (1982) 'Fear and pain in dentistry', *Bulletin of the British Psychological Society*, 35, pp. 225–8.

Lindsay, S.J.E. and Woolgrove, J. (1989) 'Attracting patients to dentists', *British Medical Journal*, 298, pp. 273–4.

Lindsay, S.J.E., Wege, P. and Yates, J. (1984) 'Expectations of sensations, discomfort and fear in dental treatment', *Behaviour Research and Therapy*, 22, pp. 99–108.

McAmmond, D.M., Davidson, P.O. and Kovitz, D.M. (1971) 'A comparison of the effects of hypnosis and relaxation training on stress reactions in a dental situation', *American Journal of Clinical Hypnosis*, 13, pp. 233–42.

Melamed, B.G. (1979) 'Behavioural approaches to fear in dental settings', *Progress in Behaviour Modifications*, 7, pp. 171–203.

Milgrom, P., Weinstein, P., Kleinknecht, R. and Getz, T. (1985) *Treating Fearful Dental Patients: A Patient Management Handbook*, Reston: Reston Publishing Company.

Murray, P., Liddell, A. and Donohue, J. (1989) 'A longitudinal study of the contribution of dental experience to dental anxiety in children between 9 and 12 years of age', *Journal of Behavioural Medicine*, 12, pp. 309–20.

Nietzel, M.T., Bernstein, D.A. and Russell, R.L. (1988) 'Assessment of anxiety and fear', **in** A.S. Bellack and M. Hersen (Eds.) *Behavioural Assessment: A Practical Handbook*, New York: Permagon Press.

Reber, A.S. (1985) *The Penguin Dictionary of Psychology*, Harmondsworth: Penguin.

Schuurs, A.H.B., Duivenvoorden, H. van Velzen, S. and Verhage, F. (1981) *Factors Associated with Regularity of Dental Attendance: An Empirical-Psychological Investigation*, Brussels: Stafleu & Tholen.

Sermet, O. (1974) 'Emotional and medical factors in child dental anxiety', *Journal of Clinical Psychology and Psychiatry*, 15, pp. 313–21.

Thrash, W.J., Marr, J.N. and Box, S.E. (1982) 'Effects of continuous patient information in the dental environment', *Journal of Dental Research*, 61, pp. 1063–5.

Wardle, J. (1982) 'Fear of dentistry', *British Journal of Medical Psychology*, 55, pp. 119–26.

10

THE MAN WHO HAS MEMORISED THE PHONE BOOK, AND OTHER STORIES

1 As noted in the text, students should have found their imagined estimate to be more accurate. Higbee (1989) suggests two possible reasons as to why visual imagery can improve memory for verbal material, and these may be considered to be complementary rather than competitive. First, it could be that visual images are inherently more memorable than words alone (Paivio & Casapo, 1973). Second, images may be processed in both a verbal and non-verbal location in the brain (Clark & Paivio, 1987), resulting in a greater likelihood of their being recalled. This 'dual coding' approach has some empirical support. Data exist which indicate that the right cerebral hemisphere plays a major role in visual imagery, whilst the left plays a major role in the verbal process (Ley, 1983).

It is also likely that concrete words (such as 'apple') are better able to produce mental images than abstract words (such as 'nourishment'). Additionally, concrete words may be processed by, and represented in, both the visual system and the verbal system. Abstract words may be processed by, and represented in, the verbal system only. According to Higbee (1989), the procedure for storing abstract words in imaginal form is the same as that for concrete words, with the exception that a step is added using 'substitution words'. Thus, a concrete word is substituted to represent the abstract word.

This can be achieved by using objects (such as a smiling face) that typify the abstract terms (such as 'happiness'). Alternatively, objects whose name sounds like the abstract word can be used. For example, 'celery' could be used for 'salary'. This 'substitution word' technique is part of the 'key' or 'link' word mnemonic method which is considered in detail in **5** below. Students should be able to recognise the limitations of the substitution word technique: the substituted word is only a *cue* to remind the person of the abstract word. The substitution word may be remembered without the person being able to remember the word it represents! Another limitation is that it is sometimes difficult to substitute good concrete words for some abstract words, and an inordinate amount of time may be spent searching for suitable substitutions. Students could try to generate a concrete word for 'assertion' to illustrate this!

2 Bizarre images are more striking and therefore more vivid than more plausible images. Additionally, they tend to be more distinctive or novel than plausible images, and take more time to form. The extra time and effort in constructing a bizarre image may help it to be remembered better.

'Interaction' and 'vividness' are two other factors that can help to make visual associations more effective. 'Interaction' means that the to-be-remembered items need to be pictured interacting in some way. For example, 'dog' and 'broom' would be better remembered if the dog was imagined sweeping with a broom rather than merely sitting next to a broom (Key & Nakayama, 1984). It is possible that interacting imagery is effective because images of separate items are combined into a single image that is remembered as a unit, with the result that each part of the image acts as a cue for the rest of it.

'Vividness' refers to an image which is 'clear, distinct, and strong' (Higbee, 1989). A person trying to remember 'dog' and 'broom', for example, should try to *picture* the two items rather than just thinking of a dog sweeping with a broom. Vividness itself is enhanced by *motion* (seeing the picture in action), *substitution* (seeing one item in place of another), *exaggeration* (seeing one or both items exaggerated in size or number) and *familiarity* (using images which are familiar in terms of previous experiences).

As far as 'bizarreness' is concerned, the evidence concerning its effectiveness is actually mixed, contrary to Lorayne and Lucas' (1974) assertions! Some studies have found that bizarre images are more effective than plausible images, some have found no differences, and a few have found that plausible images are more effective than bizarre images (Einstein & McDaniel, 1987). If bizarreness is effective, it is probably because it incorporates other factors. For example, some interacting images 'may almost have to be bizarre in order to involve interaction ... It is hard to think of a plausible picture showing an elephant and a piano interacting' (Higbee, 1989).

The paired-associates learning task is typically used in imagery studies. Usually, one group of participants is instructed to use verbal techniques to associate the to-be-remembered items whilst the other is instructed to form images linking them together. For example, if the to-be-remembered words are 'cat' and 'brick', a cat might be imagined using bricks to build a house. Students could no doubt think of a much more bizarre relationship between the cat and the brick! Research indicates that people who do use imagery remember words far more effectively than non-imagers.

One confounding effect that is known to occur in such studies is the spontaneous use of imagery by those instructed to use verbal techniques. As a result, the effectiveness of imagery is probably even stronger than is indicated by the experimental data. One individual difference that would need to be controlled for is a person's ability to form images: people who report vivid visual imagery perform better than those who report poor visual imagery (Sutherland, Harrell & Isaacs, 1987).

3 There are several possible ways of overcoming, or at least reducing, interference effects. It is possible that rather than using just one locus, orators constructed multiple sets of locations (perhaps seven sets, each representing a day of the week on which a speech was to be delivered). The orators may also have used 'progressive elaboration'. This involves adding to a progressive picture each subsequent item to be remembered at a particular location. For example, if the word 'swing' had previously been stored in a location, the new word to be stored would be imagined interacting with the swing in the same location. Evidence suggests that progressive elaboration is effective in reducing interference (Bower & Reitman, 1973), though whether this technique is more effective than using multiple sets of loci seems to be a matter of personal preference.

In order to remember a sequence of playing cards, Dominic O'Brien, who retained his championship at the Second World Memory Championships (August 7–8, 1993, Simpson's Restaurant, The Strand, London) uses a mnemonic system in which each card initially becomes a pair of initials, and then a person. The three of Clubs, for example, is 'C.C.', which then becomes Charlie Chaplin twirling a cane. The method of loci is then used to deposit the 52 people in 52 locations. O'Brien puts his previously learnt material into what he terms a 'mental video', which clears the loci for future use.

One way to store more items is to increase the number of loci within the existing loci. In the case of **6** below, six distinctive locations in each room could be visualised. An alternative approach would be to extend the loci by 'leaving the house' and imagining taking a walk down a street or to another building. Yet another approach would be to use a variant of the progressive elaboration method described above; the person could imagine six items interacting in each of the loci. The order of recall of the six items could, however, be far more difficult.

One tactic that users of the loci method employ is what Higbee (1989) terms 'distinguishing marks' for every nth location (where n is a multiple of a base number). For example, the fifth location might be pictured with a five-fingered hand, whilst the tenth might be pictured with the Prime Minister in it (10, Downing Street). The eleventh item would be recalled more quickly by going directly to the tenth location and working from there.

4 Rhyming almost certainly works by imposing meaning on material that is not inherently meaningful. A word that rhymes with one that has to be remembered acts as a cue to help the recall of it. The rhythm that accompanies a rhyme is also helpful. In the rhyme '30 days hath September', rhythm would be lost if the second line was 'April, June and May'. Acronyms and acrostics 'chunk' information. Thus, only one word has to be remembered rather than several. Meaning is also imposed on the material. Thus, 'Richard of York gave battle in vain' is a meaningful sentence whereas 'red orange yellow', and so on, is not. The methods do not store the original information, but provide cues to help retrieve it and indicate how many items needs to be recalled. In some cases, however, the first letter might not be a sufficient cue and the method does not work! The evidence suggests that acronyms and acrostics are more useful for terms with which the learner is already familiar (Morris & Cook, 1978).

5 It might be possible for students to construct a rhyme or an acronym. However, the verbal mnemonic technique that lends itself better to this task is probably the acrostic. One acrostic is as follows, 'men very easily make jugs serve useful nocturnal purposes'. Another is, 'my vehicle enables more journeys safely undertaken normally prompt'. No doubt students can generate many others. The evidence suggests that an acrostic is more effective if it has been generated by a person rather than imposed on him/her (Dickel & Slak, 1983). This could be because more effort is made in generating one's own mnemonic and/or one's own mnemonics are far more meaningful to one's self.

6 Bower (1973) offers the following:

> At the *oil factory* (olfactory nerve), the *optician* (optic) looked for the *occupant* (oculomotor) of the *truck* (trochlear). He was searching because *three gems* (trigeminal) had been *abducted* (abducens) by a man who was hiding his *face* (facial) and *ears* (auditory). A *glossy photograph* (glossopharyngeal) had been taken of him, but it was too *vague* (vagus) to use. He also appeared to be *spineless* (spinal accessory) and *hypocritical* (hypoglossal).

Students should be able to generate their own, possibly better, mnemonic. Amongst other things, the method can also be used for remembering speeches. Hanks and Belliston (1980) describe Mark Twain's impressive use of the method:

> First a haystack with a wiggly line under it to represent a rattlesnake – to remind him to begin talking about ranch life in the West. Then there were slanting lines with what must be an umbrella under them and the Roman numeral II. That referred to a great wind that would strike Carson City every afternoon at 2 o'clock.
>
> Next came a couple of jagged lines, lightning, obviously, telling him it was time to move on to the subject of weather in San Francisco, where the point was that there wasn't any lightning, or thunder either, he noted.
>
> From that day, Twain spoke without notes, and the system never failed him. He drew a picture of each section of his speech, all strung out in a row, then he'd look at them and destroy them. When he spoke, there was the row of images fresh and sharp in his mind. He'd make notes based on the remarks of a previous speaker – just insert another picture in the set of images.

7 Tomoyori could be using virtually any of the methods previously described and evaluated. Students could discuss the plausibility of the following suggestions. Tomoyori may, for example, be using some sort of pattern in the material which makes it more meaningful (Katona, 1940). He might be using some form of rhyme. However, remembering a 40 000-word rhyme would be no mean feat in and of itself! Another method could be the 'narrative story' or the 'phonetic' mnemonic system (Slak, 1971). The possibilities are very large indeed, and this **Talking point** lends itself well to a discussion among students as to the plausibility of the various mnemonic methods with such a large volume of to-be-remembered material.

What motivates Tomoyori, Carvello, O'Brien and others is, of course, a matter of speculation. However, Dominic O'Brien has been banned from playing the card game 'Blackjack' in nearly every casino in England and France. His ability to remember the cards that have been played give him an obvious advantage. In his own words, 'I started making a living out of it, winning maybe £400–£600 a week, but then I got greedy, and started making £1000 a day.' The opportunity to 'earn' money may therefore be one motivator, but it is hard to see how knowing pi to 40 000 decimal places would lead to this (save for appearances on TV magic shows).

At the 1993 Memoriad, Creighton Carvello (who finished fourth) revealed that he had memorised 5 000 telephone numbers from the Yellow Pages telephone directory, which he presumably thinks is a useful enterprise! Perhaps there is a certain kudos in being able to remember things which, as the article suggests, most people would merely look up or write down. Whether it is socially painful and personally embarrassing to have a poor memory is also a matter for debate. Newspaper adverts (e.g. 'IQ of 145 and can't remember?') certainly play on the possibility.

8 The finding that skilled chess players perform no better than novices when the pieces are arranged randomly is important in understanding their advantage when the pieces are arranged in a real game. Patterns are almost certainly being used by the skilled players in order to construct an understanding of the structure of the material. According to de Groot (1966), chess players are able to perceive the board as an organised whole rather than a collection of pieces. When the pieces are randomly arranged, the board cannot be organised into a meaningful whole and hence the chess player's advantage disappears. A useful discussion of the practical applications of memory can be found in Gruneberg and Morris (1992).

References

Bower, G.H. (1973) 'How to ... uh ... remember!' *Psychology Today*, October, pp. 63–70.

Bower, G.H. and Reitman, J.S. (1973) 'Elaboration and multilist learning', *Journal of Verbal Learning and Verbal Behaviour*, 11, pp. 478–85.

Clark, J.M. and Paivio, A. (1987) 'A dual coding perspective on encoding processes', **in** M.A. McDaniel and M. Pressley *Imagery and Related Mnemonic Processes: Theories, Individual Differences, and Applications*, New York: Springer-Verlag.

de Groot, A. (1966) 'Perception and memory versus thought: some old ideas and recent findings', **in** B. Kleinmontz (Ed.) *Problem Solving*, New York: Wiley.

Dickel, M. and Slak, S. (1983) 'Imagery vividness and memory for verbal material', *Journal of Mental Imagery*, 7, pp. 121–6.

Einstein, G. and McDaniel, M.A. (1987) 'Distinctiveness and the mnemonic benefits of bizarre imagery', **in** M.A. McDaniel and M. Pressley (Eds.) *Imagery and Related Mnemonic Processes: Theories, Individual Differences and Applications*, New York: Springer-Verlag.

Gruneberg, M. and Morris, P.E. (Eds.) (1992) *Aspects of Memory: The Practical Aspects*, London: Routledge.

Hanks, K. and Belliston, L. (1980) *Rapid Viz: A New Method for the Rapid Visualization of Ideas*, Los Altos, California: William Kaufman.

Higbee, K.L. (1989) *Your Memory: How it Works and How to Improve it*, London: Piatkus.

Katona, G. (1940) *Organizing and Memorizing: Studies in the Psychology of Learning and Teaching*, New York: Columbia University Press.

Key, D.W. and Nakayama, S.Y. (1980) 'Automatic elaborative coding in children's associative memory', *Bulletin of the Psychonomic Society*, 16, 287–90.

Ley, R.G. (1983) 'Cerebral laterality and imagery', **in** A.A. Sheikh (Ed.) *Imagery, Current Theory, Research and Application*, New York: Wiley.

Lorayne, H. and Lucas, J. (1974) *The Memory Book*, Briarcliff Manor, N.Y.: Stein & Day.

Morris, P.E. and Cook, N. (1978) 'When do first-letter mnemonics aid recall?', *British Journal of Educational Psychology*, 48, pp. 22–28.

Paivio, A. and Csapo, K. (1973) 'Picture superiority in free recall: Imagery or dual coding?' *Cognitive Psychology*, 5, pp. 176–206.

Slak, S. (1971) 'Long-term retention of random sequence digital information with the aid of phonemic recoding: a case report', *Perceptual and Motor Skills*, 33, pp. 455–60.

Sutherland, M.E., Harrell, J.P. and Isaacs, C. (1987) 'The stability of individual differences in imagery ability', *Journal of Mental Imagery*, 11, pp. 97–104.